The Enlightenment

An Enthralling Guide to a Period of Scientific, Political, and Philosophical Discourse in European History

© **Copyright 2023 - All rights reserved.**

The content contained within this book may not be reproduced, duplicated, or transmitted without direct written permission from the author or the publisher.

Under no circumstances will any blame or legal responsibility be held against the publisher, or author, for any damages, reparation, or monetary loss due to the information contained within this book, either directly or indirectly.

Legal Notice:

This book is copyright protected. It is only for personal use. You cannot amend, distribute, sell, use, quote, or paraphrase any part, or the content within this book, without the consent of the author or publisher.

Disclaimer Notice:

Please note the information contained within this document is for educational and entertainment purposes only. All effort has been executed to present accurate, up-to-date, reliable, and complete information. No warranties of any kind are declared or implied. Readers acknowledge that the author is not engaging in the rendering of legal, financial, medical, or professional advice. The content within this book has been derived from various sources. Please consult a licensed professional before attempting any techniques outlined in this book.

By reading this document, the reader agrees that under no circumstances is the author responsible for any losses, direct or indirect, that are incurred as a result of the use of the information contained within this document, including, but not limited to, errors, omissions, or inaccuracies.

Free limited time bonus

Stop for a moment. We have a free bonus set up for you. The problem is this: we forget 90% of everything that we read after 7 days. Crazy fact, right? Here's the solution: we've created a printable, 1-page pdf summary for this book that you're reading now. All you have to do to get your free pdf summary is to go to the following website:

https://livetolearn.lpages.co/enthrallinghistory/

Once you do, it will be intuitive. Enjoy, and thank you!

Table of Contents

INTRODUCTION 1
CHAPTER 1 - BEFORE THE ENLIGHTENMENT 3
CHAPTER 2 - MONUMENTAL RISE OF ENLIGHTENED PHILOSOPHY... 14
CHAPTER 3 - HOW SCIENCE CHANGED THE WORLD........................... 20
CHAPTER 4 - AMBITIOUS LUST FOR ABSOLUTE POWER 32
CHAPTER 5 - CORE PILLARS OF ENLIGHTENED THOUGHT 44
CHAPTER 6 - INTELLECTUAL TITANS WHO CHANGED THE COURSE OF HISTORY 53
CHAPTER 7 - WOMEN WHO DEFIED THE LIMITS OF THEIR TIME 67
CHAPTER 8 - THE AMERICAN ENLIGHTENMENT 75
CHAPTER 9 - QUEST FOR LIBERTY AND EQUALITY 84
CONCLUSION 92
HERE'S ANOTHER BOOK BY ENTHRALLING HISTORY THAT YOU MIGHT LIKE... 95
FREE LIMITED TIME BONUS.. 96
BIBLIOGRAPHY 97

Introduction

This book will take you on a journey to a time that changed the world's political, social, and cultural fabric. The Enlightenment started at the end of the 17th century and lasted until the beginning of the 19th century. There was a significant shift in thinking, as prominent intellectuals and philosophers began to challenge traditional sources of authority and knowledge. They embraced reason, science, and progress, paving the way for a new era of freedom and democracy.

The Enlightenment, which primarily took shape in Europe, was a pivotal moment in the history of ideas. It was a time of monumental intellectual upheaval based on the belief in human reason, a desire for progress, and a need for social, political, and economic reforms. The impact of Enlightenment ideas is significant and long-lasting, as they shaped our understanding of democracy, individualism, equality, and human rights.

This book will delve into several aspects of this period and learn about its central themes and ideas. We will also look at its key figures and institutions and their impact on today's world.

We aim to provide an overview of this critical period of history while explaining its relevance to contemporary issues and debates. What sets this volume apart from others is its construction of the Enlightenment. Rather than treating the period as a massive unified movement, we'll focus on the diversity of views and conflicts that characterized it.

Our goal is to bring you knowledge and provide vivid descriptions of the people, places, and events that shaped this fascinating era. You'll meet the greatest thinkers and visionaries of the age, from Voltaire and Rousseau to Locke and Hume. You'll witness the birth of democracy and the fight for human rights and see how the Enlightenment paved the way for the world we know today.

We will attempt to break down barriers and make knowledge accessible to people from all walks of life. The ideas and events of this period are too important to be confined to the ivory towers of academia. Everyone should have the opportunity to explore and understand the Enlightenment.

To achieve this, we've taken great care to present history in a clear and accessible manner, using simple language and providing examples that are easy to follow and understand. We have avoided engaging in esoteric debates and using technical jargon, focusing instead on the major themes, ideas, and events that defined the era. History books can often be dull and difficult to read, so we have worked hard to make this book interesting and entertaining, with plenty of real-life stories and anecdotes that bring the history of the Enlightenment to life.

We believe that history is not just a recitation of dry facts and figures but a rich tapestry of stories and experiences that can captivate and inspire us all. Whether you are a student of history or simply curious about the origins of modernity, this book will provide a roadmap for a better understanding of the Enlightenment era.

We invite you to join us on this fascinating journey of discovery and to experience the power and drama of the Enlightenment era.

Enjoy.

Chapter 1 – Before the Enlightenment

As the sun set over the grand old buildings and monuments of Paris, the city's finest minds gathered in a dimly lit salon, their voices hushed as they discussed the latest ideas racing across Europe. With its heady mix of reason, science, and philosophy, the Enlightenment swept through the salons and coffeehouses of Europe like wildfire, igniting a passion for knowledge and freedom in the hearts of all who dared to dream of a better world.

From Voltaire's biting satire to Rousseau's passionate pleas for justice, from Newton's laws of motion to Descartes's cogito, ergo sum ("I think, therefore I am"), the Enlightenment opened minds and challenged established ideas in ways never before seen. And as the people of Paris spilled out into the streets, eager to seize the day and embrace the future, a sense of excitement and possibility hung in the air like a beacon in the darkness, signaling all who dared to follow.

The Enlightenment was an intellectual and cultural movement in the 17th and 18th centuries characterized by a focus on reason, individualism, and skepticism toward traditional authority. But before the Enlightenment, Europe experienced several incredible events and cultural movements that shaped how society was organized and operated.

The Middle Ages

The Middle Ages lasted from the 5th to the 15th century and was a time of great upheaval and change. These were not happy times, as the masses typically suffered during this period. It was a time of feudalism, where kings and lords held power over their vassals. The majority of people lived in rural areas. Wars and diseases affected their lives, making them miserable.

The Middles Ages is typically seen as starting in 476 CE when the Western Roman Empire fell to the Germanic leader Odoacer, who staged a revolt and deposed Emperor Romulus Augustulus. Europe went into a period of chaos.

Barbarian hordes swept across the continent, destroying everything in their path. The once-great city of Rome was destroyed, and the people of Europe were left without anyone to defend them from these invaders.

But from the ashes of the old world rose a new one. The Carolingian dynasty, led by the great emperor Charlemagne, emerged in the 8th century. He built an empire that spanned the length and breadth of Western Europe and began to re-establish order in the region.

But this did not last long. Eventually, Europe became one large religious state. Although there were many kingdoms in Europe, they had one thing in common; they were all Catholic. The spiritual hierarchy and the secular rulers had to find a way to share the power, each wanting more.

The Catholic Church played a key role, as it was the supreme authority. The pope was (and still is) the head of the Catholic Church, and he could make life very difficult for the rulers who wanted to go against him. Some kings tried to restrict church activities, and the church, in turn, attempted to control the affairs of the state, even going as far as to excommunicate those who disagreed.

For the most part, though, people clung to their faith. Priests toiled to preserve the knowledge of the ancients. The cathedrals of Europe rose, reaching toward the heavens. The church was a powerful force that provided stability and the foundation for social cohesion.

As you can see, the Middle Ages presents a confusing and often contradictory picture of a society attempting to structure itself politically on a spiritual basis. And this was a time of contradictions and extremes, a time of incredible beauty and terrible brutality. But through it all, the people of Europe endured, clinging to hope and faith for a better tomorrow.

The Renaissance

The Renaissance emerged in the 14th century and lasted until the 17th century. It was a period of cultural and artistic rebirth marked by a renewed interest in classical learning, literature, and the arts. Historians have identified several causes for the emergence of the Renaissance following the Middle Ages, such as increased interaction between different cultures, the rediscovery of ancient Greek and Roman texts, humanism, and various artistic and technological innovations.

Humanism emphasizes the value of human life and achievements. It is an approach to a life based on reason and common humanity, recognizing that moral values are founded in human nature and experience alone.

Italy, the birthplace of the Renaissance, celebrated the power and potential of the individual to achieve greatness. Scholars and artists rediscovered the ancient wisdom of Greece and Rome and infused it with their passion and vision. Painters like Leonardo da Vinci, Michelangelo, and Raphael created works of breathtaking beauty and splendor, capturing the human form and spirit with a vividness and intensity never before seen.

Meanwhile, scientists like Galileo, Copernicus, and Newton challenged the church's traditional beliefs. They opened up new vistas of understanding the universe and our place in it. These scientists changed our understanding of astronomy, mathematics, and physics. They laid the framework for the Scientific Revolution, which would transform the world forever.

But the Renaissance was not just a time of intellectual and artistic achievements. A great upheaval was also taking place in the social and political circles. The old feudal system was winding down with the rise of the middle class, the development of new forms of government, and the growth of the banking sectors.

And in the end, the Renaissance left a profound legacy that continues to shape our world today. It gave birth to the idea of individualism and the belief that we have the power to shape our destiny and achieve greatness. It fostered a spirit of innovation, inquiry, and creativity that has driven human progress ever since. And it provided a model of beauty, wisdom, and harmony that has inspired generations of artists, scientists, and thinkers to reach for the stars and achieve the impossible.

The Reformation

The Reformation took place in the 16th century. This religious movement challenged the authority of the Catholic Church, leading to the formation of Protestantism. It was a time of religious and social upheaval, as people questioned the power of the Catholic Church and sought new ways to connect with God.

At the heart of the Reformation was a burning sense of moral outrage and spiritual longing. Many people felt the Catholic Church had become a bloated, corrupt institution that cared more about power and wealth than the spiritual well-being of its followers. They saw the Vatican's opulence and the clergy's decadence as a betrayal of the faith of the early Christians.

As a result, a group of bold and visionary reformers emerged. These thinkers were determined to restore what they believed were the actual teachings of Christ and create a more authentic form of Christianity. The fiery and charismatic Martin Luther led the charge.

In 1517, Martin Luther published a document called Disputation on the Power of Indulgences, better known as the Ninety-five Theses. This document outlined ninety-five issues about the Catholic Church's teachings.

We won't cover all ninety-five theses, but one of the most critical issues, at least in Luther's view, was the Catholic Church's role as an intermediary between the people and God. The Catholic Church allowed people to purchase indulgences to forgive their sins and reduce their time in purgatory. Luther argued against this practice, believing instead that salvation was a gift God gave to those with faith.

He also believed that believers should be less dependent on the Catholic Church and its pope and priests for spiritual guidance. People should have an independent relationship with God, take personal responsibility for their faith, and refer to the Bible for spiritual guidance.

This Reformation quickly spread throughout Europe, sparking a wave of religious and political conflicts. The movement formed a new sect of Christianity called Protestantism. This name refers collectively to the many religious groups that separated from the Roman Catholic Church due to differences in practices and beliefs.

The Scientific Revolution

The Reformation brought about a change in religious thought, and the Scientific Revolution brought about a change in how people acquired knowledge. People's thinking about the natural world changed dramatically between the 16th and 17th centuries. It was characterized by a shift away from traditional beliefs and toward the use of reason and observation.

Francis Bacon

One of the key figures of the Scientific Revolution was Francis Bacon, an English philosopher, statesman, and scientist who lived from 1561 to 1626. Few individuals can compare intellectually to this great man.

Bacon's dedication to the pursuit of knowledge was legendary. He believed science should be based on empirical evidence and that experiments and observations should be used to test theories. His approach to science was revolutionary. He emphasized collecting data and conducting experiments to verify or disprove scientific hypotheses.

Galileo Galilei

Another important figure of the Scientific Revolution was Galileo Galilei. He was a brilliant Italian astronomer, physicist, and mathematician who dared to challenge the prevailing beliefs of his time. His scientific contributions are still relevant today, even after more than four hundred years.

For instance, his work on mechanics laid the foundations for the modern study of physics, including the principle of inertia. He improved the telescope's design and made groundbreaking observations of the moon, the phases of Venus, and the moons of Jupiter, providing evidence for the heliocentric model of the solar system proposed by Copernicus. Heliocentrism claims that the sun is the center of the universe.

However, Galileo's support for this revolutionary idea directly conflicted with the powerful Catholic Church, which held that the Earth was the center of the universe. Galileo refused to back down and continued to pursue his scientific investigations. After the publication of the Dialogue Concerning the Two Chief World System in 1632, Galileo was ordered to appear before an inquisition in Rome. He was charged with heresy for his belief that the sun was at the center of the universe.

To avoid being killed, Galileo agreed not to spread that teaching anymore. As he was being taken away, he allegedly mumbled, "Eppur si muove (And yet it moves)." Galileo spent the rest of his life under house arrest.

Isaac Newton

Isaac Newton was born in England in 1643. Newton was a prodigious child who would become one of history's most brilliant scientific minds. His contributions to science were nothing short of awe-inspiring.

He is best known for his theory of universal gravitation and made an incredible contribution by formulating calculus, a new branch of mathematics. He also made significant advancements in mechanics, optics, and chemical research.

Newton became a dominant scientific force in Britain following the publication of his book Principia in 1687. The three laws of motion and the principle of universal gravitation he proposed helped explain why the planets orbit around the sun and why objects fall to the ground. His groundbreaking body of work, known as Newtonian Mechanics, is still taught in schools today. The publication of this work is typically used as the end date for the Scientific Revolution. The lines between the Scientific Revolution and the Enlightenment blur a little. We chose not to cage individuals like Newton and Descartes to only one movement, as their ideas inspired thinkers during both.

Newton's ideas and discoveries laid the foundations for some of the most important scientific and technological discoveries to come. He was a trailblazer and visionary thinker who challenged the prevailing beliefs of his time to explore the unknown with fearless curiosity.

René Descartes

René Descartes was a French philosopher and mathematician. He believed in the power of reason and thought that knowledge could only be gained through careful reasoning and skepticism.

Descartes believed in a radical approach to knowledge that rejected the authority of tradition and emphasized the importance of individual reasoning and experimentation. He is famous for his statement, "Cogito, ergo sum" ("I think, therefore I am"), which encapsulates his belief that our ability to reason is the foundation of all knowledge. Descartes was also a mathematician and is considered "the father of analytical geometry. He will be mentioned again because his philosophical ideas greatly impacted Enlightenment thinkers.

Political and Social Thinkers

Political and social thinkers also contributed to the rise of Enlightenment ideals. John Locke and Jean-Jacques Rousseau were just two figures who put forward the importance of individual freedom and social and political reforms. Their ideas challenged traditional forms of government and social organizations. They helped pave the way for new political and social systems based on reason, justice, and human rights. We will examine these thinkers more closely in another chapter. Still, they are important to mention here since they significantly impacted the rise and spread of the Enlightenment.

Growth of Trade and Commerce

The growth of commerce and trade played a role in the Enlightenment. As Europe became more interconnected through trade and business, people were exposed to new ideas and perspectives from different cultures. This exposure to new ways of thinking helped fuel the Enlightenment's emphasis on reason and progress.

The Printing Press Was the Key to the Enlightenment

The printing press was the most important invention in spreading the ideas of the Enlightenment. Although the printing press had been around for centuries in China, the new, improved printing press developed by Johannes Gutenberg in the mid-15th century helped to disseminate ideas and information more widely and rapidly than ever before. Before the printing press, books were primarily produced by hand, which made them expensive and difficult to produce in large quantities. As a result, access to advanced knowledge was mostly limited to a small group of elites, such as wealthy aristocrats, religious leaders, and scholars.

Gutenberg's improved printing press made it possible to mass-produce books and other printed materials at a much lower cost and with greater speed than before, allowing them to reach a much broader audience. Before the invention of printing, the number of books in Europe could be counted in thousands. By 1500, after only fifty years of the creation of the improved printing press, more than nine million books had been published. Since books became cheaper and more readily available, the middle class could access them, which led to an exponential increase in literacy rates.

The first books created on Gutenberg's printing press were religious texts, such as the Gutenberg Bible, printed in Mainz, Germany, in the

1450s. After the success of the Gutenberg Bible, other religious texts were printed using the new technology. The first books published in English were also religious texts, such as other Bibles, hymns, and psalms.

The famous astronomer Johannes Kepler wrote some of the first science books printed on the printing press. In 1609, Kepler published Astronomia Nova (New Astronomy), which outlined his three major laws of planetary motion:

(1) The planets move in elliptical orbits with the sun at one focus.

(2) The time necessary to traverse any arc of a planetary orbit is proportional to the area of the sector between the central body and that arc.

(3) An exact relationship exists between the squares of the planets' periodic times and the cubes of their mean distances from the sun.

This text was followed by Harmonices Mundi (The Harmony of the World) in 1619, which explores the mathematical relationships between planetary motion and music.

Another notable scientific work was Nicolaus Copernicus's De revolutionibus orbium coelestium (On the Revolutions of the Celestial Spheres), published in 1543. This work proposed the heliocentric model of the solar system, with the sun at the center and the planets orbiting around it.

Galileo Galilei's Sidereus Nuncius (Starry Messenger), published in 1610, described his observations of the moons of Jupiter, and William Harvey's De motu cordis (On the Motion of the Heart), published in 1628, described his discovery of the circulation of blood in the human body.

The printing press played a crucial role in unlocking the Enlightenment. First, it made it possible for Enlightenment thinkers to publish and spread their ideas more widely, allowing them to reach a larger audience. It also facilitated the creation of a public sphere where people could freely exchange ideas and opinions, leading to new forms of political and cultural discourse. Finally, it helped to break down the traditional barriers to knowledge, making information more widely available to people from all walks of life.

The Major Ideas of the Enlightenment

These ideas and values helped to pave the way for the Enlightenment by providing a framework for new ways of thinking and understanding the world.

Let's lay out the most important ideas of the Enlightenment. The reason was perhaps the most prevalent and influential Enlightenment idea. Enlightenment thinkers believed people could understand and improve the world through reason and scientific inquiry. These thinkers rejected superstition, dogma, and traditional authority, instead emphasizing critical thinking and rationality. They sought to create a more just and equal society and advocated for democracy, freedom of speech, and religious tolerance.

Individualism was another feature of the Enlightenment. Enlightenment thinkers rejected the traditional authority of the Church and the Divine Right of kings, instead championing the rights of the individual. They believed that all people were equal and everyone had the right to pursue their interests and goals. Individualism helped to create a more liberal and democratic society. Different thinkers had different views on who was equal. For instance, Rousseau did not believe women were equal to men, while Locke believed women could rationalize just like men.

Enlightenment thinkers valued the scientific method and believed knowledge could be gained through observation and experimentation. They thought science was the key to understanding the natural world and solving many problems plaguing society. This emphasis on science led to discoveries and advancements, helping shape their understanding of the world.

Did People Easily Embrace the Enlightenment?

The popularity of the Enlightenment varied depending on the time and place. The Enlightenment was a widely influential movement in Europe that significantly impacted society, politics, and culture. Enlightenment ideas and values spread through various channels, including academic institutions, literary works, and salons where intellectuals gathered to exchange ideas.

A painting of a salon. The men have gathered to listen to Voltaire's latest work.
https://en.wikipedia.org/wiki/File:Salon_de_Madame_Geoffrin.jpg

However, not everyone embraced the Enlightenment. Many conservative forces, such as the church and the monarchy, saw the beliefs of many Enlightenment thinkers threatening their power. They sought to suppress its ideas through censorship and persecution of intellectuals.

There were also significant regional differences in the popularity and impact of the Enlightenment, with some countries and regions, such as France and Germany, seeing a powerful influence.

The understanding of the Enlightenment varied widely among different segments of society. While Enlightenment ideas significantly impacted intellectual and cultural elites, not everyone could fully grasp the complex philosophical and scientific concepts associated with the movement.

Despite these challenges, the ideas of the Enlightenment had a significant impact on Western culture and society, particularly in science, politics, and philosophy. The Enlightenment promoted using reason and empirical evidence to understand the world, pursue additional knowledge and education, and value individual liberty and democratic governance.

The End of an Era: Looking Forward to the Enlightenment

For all its darkness and uncertainty, the pre-Enlightenment era was a time of great creativity, innovation, and boundless imagination. From the towering spires of Gothic cathedrals to the delicate brushstrokes of Renaissance masterpieces, from the haunting melodies of troubadours to the intricate tapestries of courtly love, the pre-Enlightenment era was a rich mosaic of human achievements and a testament to the power of the human spirit to overcome the greatest of obstacles.

And so, as the last embers of the fire died away and as the night settled in around them, the people of the pre-Enlightenment world could rest easy in the knowledge that their legacy would endure, that their dreams would live on, and that the future would be brighter than they could have ever imagined.

Chapter 2 – Monumental Rise of Enlightened Philosophy

In the heart of London, a man walked briskly over the cobblestone street, his eyes fixed on the horizon. His name was Francis Bacon, and he was on a mission.

Bacon had spent his life searching for a new way of understanding the world based on logic and observation rather than superstition and tradition. And now, as he watched the sun rise over the rooftops, he knew he was making a difference. For Bacon and many other philosophers of his day, the dawn of the Enlightenment was at hand, and nothing would be the same again.

Philosophy is a discipline that has been central to human thought for thousands of years. It involves the critical study of fundamental questions of morality and life. Why are we here? What is our purpose? Philosophical insights provide a framework for critical inquiry, moral and political reasoning, and a deeper understanding of the human experience. Philosophy also plays a vital role in shaping our values and beliefs.

Francis Bacon's Empiricism

Francis Bacon, who lived from 1561 to 1626, was an English philosopher and scientist who developed a philosophical concept called empiricism, which proposed knowledge comes from sensory experiences. In other words, we can only understand the world through our senses.

Empiricism was a departure from the traditional approach to knowledge, which relied on intuition or revelation. Bacon argued that knowledge gained through observation and experimentation was more reliable than knowledge gained through abstract reasoning. Empiricism is grounded in concrete evidence and could be tested and verified through further observations and experiments. Experimentation aims to apply theories to real-world observations, record the findings as empirical data, and present them to people.

Bacon argued that everything you know and believe comes from what you can physically experience. For example, if you know that concrete is hard, it is only because you fell on a concrete floor and realized this. If you know that your father is kind, it is because he has done kind things in the past. You only know what you have experienced; anything you have not personally experienced is mere conjecture and not to be trusted.

Bacon's empiricism had a significant impact on the development of science. His emphasis on experimentation laid the foundation for the scientific method, which involves making observations, formulating hypotheses, conducting experiments to test those hypotheses, and analyzing the results. This approach to learning was seen as a powerful tool for challenging traditional ideas and superstitions and for promoting a more rational and evidence-based worldview.

Descartes's Rationalist Beliefs

One of the most famous images of Descartes.
https://en.wikipedia.org/wiki/File:Frans_Hals_-_Portret_van_Ren%C3%A9_Descartes.jpg

René Descartes lived from 1596 to 1650 and was a French philosopher, scientist, and mathematician. In 1622, Descartes moved to Paris. He was a lively fellow and enjoyed life in Paris, where he gambled, rode horses, and fenced. He attended court, concerts, and plays regularly to amuse himself.

As a philosopher, his beliefs were centered around the idea that reason and logic were the primary sources of knowledge. He believed that by using our innate capacity for reason, we could arrive at certain knowledge that was beyond doubt. Descartes argued that sensory experiences, while important, were unreliable and could not be trusted as a source for all knowledge.

One of Descartes's most famous arguments is *cogito, ergo sum* or "I think, therefore I am." He argued that the very act of thinking and doubting was proof of one's existence. Descartes used this argument as a foundation for his philosophy, arguing that reason and logic could be used to arrive at other certain truths about the world.

Descartes's rationalist beliefs also included the idea of innate ideas, which he believed were present in the mind from birth. According to Descartes, these innate ideas were the foundation of all knowledge. He thought that the mind could understand complex concepts and that this understanding was not dependent on sensory experiences.

The three innate ideas he believed in were the following:

(1) The idea of God who is perfect and infinite.
(2) The idea of self or mind, which he expressed in his famous phrase "*Cogito, ergo sum.*"
(3) The idea of infinity and some other mathematical truths. According to Descartes, these ideas could not come from experience but are present in the human mind from birth.

Another key aspect of Descartes's rationalist beliefs was his emphasis on the importance of deductive reasoning. He believed that by starting with fundamental truths and using deductive reasoning, one could arrive at new knowledge that could not be refuted. This approach to learning was in contrast to the sensory-based approach advocated by empiricists.

Descartes's deductive reasoning was also closely tied to the Enlightenment's commitment to the scientific method. By emphasizing the importance of starting with fundamental truths and using deductive reasoning to arrive at new knowledge, Descartes helped to lay the foundation for the evidence-based approach to science that became central to the Enlightenment's scientific and philosophical developments.

Voltaire and Rousseau: Ideas of Reason

Voltaire and Rousseau were two influential Enlightenment thinkers who championed the ancient Greek idea of reason. Both philosophers believed reason was essential to human progress and advocated for its use in every aspect of life, including politics, religion, and morality.

Voltaire, who lived from 1694 to 1778, was a French philosopher and writer best known for advocating reason, religious tolerance, and free speech. He believed that reason could be used to challenge traditional beliefs and superstitions. He also thought that reason was essential for promoting social and political progress. Voltaire was critical of the Catholic Church and its teachings, arguing they were based on superstition and fear rather than reason and evidence.

Voltaire's views on women's rights mirrored the social and cultural norms of his time. While he had some progressive ideas, such as the belief that women should have access to education, his views on women's rights were not as progressive as today. Early in his career, he believed women were inherently inferior to men physically and intellectually and that their roles should be confined to the home as mothers, daughters, and wives. His views on women changed over time. Although he held views we would see as sexist today, his thoughts on equality were revolutionary and not embraced by everyone, including other women.

Jean-Jacques Rousseau, who lived from 1712 to 1778, was a Swiss-born French philosopher and writer. Rousseau vehemently believed that reason was essential to developing an individual's mind and could be used to create a more just and equal society.

Rousseau strongly thought that individuals were equal and that everyone was born free. He believed that society must ensure everyone had access to the means to survive, live, and prosper. Like Voltaire, Rousseau also had regressive ideas about women. He believed in the natural differences between men and women. Rousseau thought women were more emotional and nurturing, making them more suitable for home life. Meanwhile, he saw men as more rational and suited for public life.

Rousseau expressed his condemnation of slavery and argued that slavery was a violation of the natural rights of man. He stated that enslaving other men went against the principles of justice and morality. He was critical of the social and political systems of his time since he believed they were corrupt and oppressive.

We will cover these four men in more depth later in the book, but you should have a clearer picture of their core beliefs. Many Enlightenment thinkers held these same beliefs or a similar version of them. These thinkers' emphasis on reason and critical thinking helped to promote a more critical and reflective attitude toward traditional beliefs and encouraged individuals to question those beliefs and develop theories based on their own reasoning.

The Counter-Enlightenment

The Counter-Enlightenment was a movement that ran against Enlightenment thinking. It developed mainly in Europe in the late 18th and early 19th centuries as a reaction against the ideas of the Enlightenment. It was not an organized movement, and there was no single catalyst for it to emerge. Instead, it is better understood as an intellectual phenomenon that ran counter to the Enlightenment.

While the Enlightenment emphasized reason, progress, individualism, and the power of science, the Counter-Enlightenment rejected those ideas and advocated for a return to traditional values, social hierarchies, and religion.

The Counter-Enlightenment was marked by a deep skepticism toward reason and the power of the human intellect. Many Counter-Enlightenment thinkers argued that human reason was limited and fallible. They believed people could not grasp the complexities of human nature and society. In their opinion, traditional forms of knowledge, such as religion, were more reliable guides to human conduct and social organization than reason and science.

The Counter-Enlightenment also rejected the Enlightenment's emphasis on progress and individualism, arguing that these values led to moral and social degradation. Many Counter-Enlightenment thinkers believed that society needed to be structured around hierarchies of power and authority, with the upper classes exercising control over the lower classes. They also emphasized the importance of social cohesion and communal values instead of individual rights and freedoms. Some prominent Counter-Enlightenment thinkers include Johann Georg

Hamann, Joseph de Maistre, and Friedrich von Schelling.

The Counter-Enlightenment's rejection of Enlightenment ideals did not find widespread acceptance among the general population, but it did impact elites. Many prominent writers, artists, and philosophers embraced the Counter-Enlightenment's critique of reason and individualism. They saw Enlightenment ideas as contributing to great upheavals in society. They did not want to mess with their traditional ways of life and advocated for a return to established values and traditional authority.

This shift in cultural and intellectual attitudes had an impact on society. The Romantic movement, which emerged in the late 18th and early 19th centuries, was a reaction against rationalism. This movement celebrated emotion, intuition, and nature instead, helping to create a cultural climate that was less receptive to Enlightenment ideas and more sympathetic to traditional values and religious orthodoxy.

Most people rejected the Counter-Enlightenment since they saw tangible benefits from the Enlightenment's emphasis on reason and progress. For example, advances in medicine, agriculture, and industry improved people's lives and made people more prosperous. The Enlightenment's emphasis on individualism and personal freedom also resonated with many people, who saw it as a way to break free from the constraints of traditional social hierarchies and allow them to pursue their own goals and aspirations.

Another reason many people rejected the Counter-Enlightenment could have been its association with religious orthodoxy and authoritarianism. The Counter-Enlightenment rejected the Enlightenment's emphasis on reason and science and sought to impose traditional values and religious dogma on society. This was seen as a threat to personal freedoms and individualism, so many people rejected the Counter-Enlightenment's ideas in favor of the more open and liberal values of the Enlightenment.

Chapter 3 – How Science Changed the World

In the early 18th century, coal miners in England encountered a formidable obstacle of how to drain water from the mines to extract coal safely and efficiently. Mines were frequently inundated with water, leading to serious fatal accidents. Horses and manual labor were used to pump water from the mines, but they were insufficient for the task. Miners desperately looked for more advanced solutions.

And this was when Thomas Newcomen intervened. He had been experimenting with steam power for years, and in 1712, he designed a machine that he believed would work. His steam engine employed a piston to drive a pump, and it was powered by steam that was generated by boiling water by burning coal.

Newcomen's engine was a marvel of ingenuity and quickly proved to be a game-changer for the coal mining industry. Miners could now pump water from the mines to extract coal at a faster and more efficient pace than ever before, and they could do so without risking their lives.

The Power of Science

A new beginning was on the horizon that would shake the very foundations of knowledge, truth, and reality and revolutionize everything in which people believed. That force was science.

As the Enlightenment gained momentum, science became ever more important, spreading its influence over all aspects of society. During the Enlightenment, people experienced immense transformation, as they finally broke free from the shackles of mysticism. They wielded the power of rationality and empirical evidence, enabling them to perceive the world in previously unfathomable ways.

In the wake of this transformation, remarkable discoveries and innovations emerged, altering the course of history. Science was no longer just a tool for comprehending the world; it became a way of life and a force capable of revolutionizing everything it touched.

The scientific discoveries of the time, including the laws of physics and chemistry and principles of biology, created a new framework for comprehending the world. This framework challenged the traditional authorities, namely the church.

Science also helped to cultivate a sense of optimism and progress. The belief in reason and the power of human ingenuity led many thinkers to believe that humanity was capable of achieving great things. New scientific discoveries and theories inspired writers, artists, and musicians to explore new themes and experiment with new forms of expression by using new tools developed during this era.

For example, author Jonathan Swift was inspired by science to write *Gulliver's Travels* in 1726, a popular novel that can be called protoscience fiction writing. Mary Wollstonecraft Shelley was an English writer who wrote *Frankenstein* in 1818, which is considered to be the first science fiction novel.

A scientific invention called the camera obscura was an optical device that makes images without a photographic film. This invention was used by artists like Johannes Vermeer and Canaletto to create more realistic paintings with better perspective, realistic colors, and lighting.

Artists Maria Sibylla Merian and John James Audubon painted detailed and scientifically accurate paintings of plants, birds, and other animals, which contributed to the dissemination of scientific information and also satisfied their artistic urges.

At the forefront of the "scientific revolution" of the Enlightenment was the scientific method, which emphasized the value of observation, testing hypotheses, and empirical evidence. This approach was groundbreaking, allowing scientists to delve deeper into the natural world and human nature. This method provided a rigorous and systematic way of understanding the world and helped to establish science as a legitimate and respected field of study.

Another significant facet of science during the Enlightenment era was an emphasis on rationalism. Enlightenment thinkers believed that the human intellect was capable of understanding the world through rationality and logic rather than depending on religious or traditional authorities to tell them why things worked the way they did. In science, the emphasis was on empirical observation and experimentation, which was a radical deviation from the past and paved the way for modern scientific advancements.

Enlightenment science was not only concerned with furthering people's comprehension of the natural world but also with enhancing and improving life and society. For instance, novel medical discoveries and treatments helped to boost public health and prolong life. Several Enlightenment thinkers believed the application of scientific knowledge could lead to progress in fields like agriculture and industry.

However, the changes science brought about were not readily accepted by everyone. Numerous religious and political authorities regarded the rise of Enlightenment science as a menace to their power and influence, and they endeavored to suppress or discredit scientific inquiries that challenged their authority.

Despite these challenges, Enlightenment science continued to flourish and spread throughout Europe and beyond. It inspired a new generation of thinkers and innovators who were propelled by a passion for discovery and dedication to the truth.

Scientific Advancements and Inventions

During the Enlightenment, numerous scientific advancements and inventions materialized that had a profound impact on various segments of society. We are going to cover some of the most important inventions that came out of the Enlightenment; a few might surprise you!

Steam Engine

Thomas Newcomen's steam engine, which he created in 1712, was quickly adopted by coal miners throughout England. Coal miners saw this invention as a lifesaver, as it could help them extract coal more efficiently and safely. However, Newcomen was never satisfied with his invention. He continued to experiment with different designs and techniques, trying to find ways to make his engine more efficient.

In the 1760s, a Scottish inventor named James Watt came across Newcomen's engine and saw the potential for improvement. Watt succeeded in building a steam engine that did not fail too often and was more reliable and efficient than the older models.

But Watt's work did not come without setbacks. He struggled for years to find the right combination of designs and materials, and he nearly gave up on several occasions. However, he persisted in his work, as he was driven by a fierce determination to create something truly revolutionary. In 1775, Watt succeeded in fabricating a new design of a steam engine that was more efficient than anything that had existed before.

The Newcomen steam engine used steam to push a cylinder with a piston connected to the shaft of the pump. The cylinder was then cooled by cold water, which created a vacuum. This moved the piston, and by repeating the cycle, a to-and-fro motion was achieved that operated the water pump.

The improvement that Watt made was in how the machine condensed steam. In Newcomen's engine, water was sprayed directly into the steam cylinder to condense the steam. The cylinder itself was heated and cooled continuously, which wasted a lot of steam by heating the cylinder on every stroke of the engine. In Watt's engine, the cylinder was opened to a separate chamber by a pipe, and cold water was sprayed into that chamber for cooling. That allowed the working cylinder to stay hot so that no steam was wasted reheating the cylinder on each stroke.

The steam engine was a groundbreaking invention, and it was used in the development of new industries, such as textile and other manufacturing industries. It also transformed the transportation industry since it powered the first locomotives and steamships, which changed the way people traveled and transported goods.

The steam engine had a profound impact on the economy and helped to transform society by creating new employment opportunities and increasing the production of goods. The steam engine had many applications in many different fields of industry, making it incredibly versatile. The Industrial Revolution, which started around 1760, would not have been the same without the steam engine.

Immunization

For many centuries, smallpox was a horrible disease that devastated humankind. Smallpox affected all levels of society. In the 18th century in Europe, 400,000 people died annually of smallpox. The disease began with a fever and a red rash that spread all over the body. The rash converted to mushy pustules that dried up and became scabs. When the scabs healed, they fell off, leaving behind large ugly pockmarks all over the skin, particularly the face. The disease had a fatality rate of 20 to 60 percent and left most survivors with horrible disfiguring facial scars. One-third of the survivors went blind.

Dr. Edward Jenner lived from 1749 to 1823. He was an English country physician who noticed that the general population was disfigured by smallpox while the milkmaids in the countryside had clear complexions. These ladies had smooth, flawless skin, their faces unscarred by the disease. Jenner observed that since the maids were in daily contact with the cow's udders while milking them, they had a mild disease they contracted from the cows called cowpox, which only left a single pustule on the hands with no other serious manifestations of the disease. Thus, these girls never acquired smallpox.

Jenner wondered if cowpox gave some protection against deadly smallpox. He decided to test the effectiveness of this method. In the summer of 1796, he extracted some gooey matter from a diseased pustule on the hand of a milkmaid. Using a syringe, he injected some of the pustule material into the forearm of his gardener's young son. The boy soon developed a scab on his arm and experienced some soreness and a mild fever for a day or so.

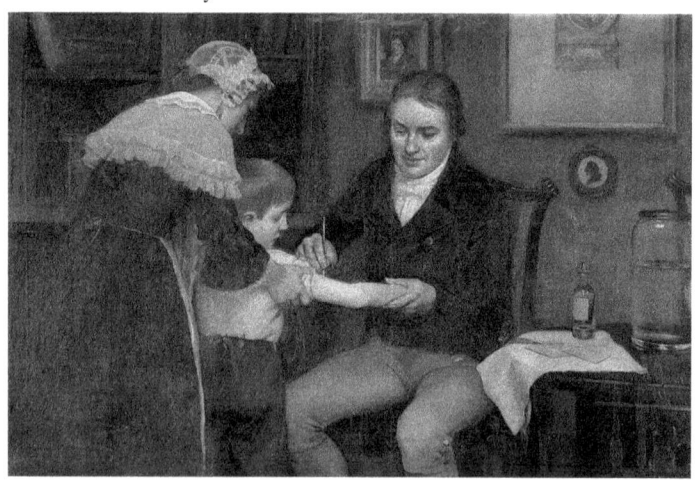

A painting of Jenner vaccinating a young boy.
https://commons.wikimedia.org/wiki/File:Jenner_phipps_01_(cropped).jpg

After about six weeks, Dr. Jenner again injected the young boy, this time with smallpox matter. As Jenner was expecting, the boy did not develop smallpox. He showed no symptoms of the disease at all. This was the first successful vaccination experiment.

Of course, such an experiment, especially one on a child, would not be allowed today. Dr. Jenner would have gone to jail had he done the experiment that way in present times. But those were different times. And thankfully for the boy (and civilization), Dr. Jenner had successfully invented vaccination. The word "vaccination" has its roots in the Latin *vacca*, meaning "cow."

Dr. Jenner published his findings about the vaccination procedure in scientific journals. Vaccination became the standard procedure for preventing people from obtaining the deadly smallpox disease.

Immunization had a significant impact on public health since it prevented many infectious diseases. As a result, the mortality rate came down drastically, and people lived healthier and longer lives.

Today, people can get vaccines against a whole host of infectious diseases, but smallpox is not one of them. Due to a global program of mass vaccination, the entire world population was officially declared free of this devastating disease in 1980.

Lightning Rod

It was a stormy day in June of 1752. Dark clouds were gathering over the city of Philadelphia. Rain was beginning to fall, and bolts of lightning streaked through the sky. People scuttled around for shelter, but not Benjamin Franklin. He was in the mood for a little kite flying. But flying kites in a storm wasn't a pastime of his; it was a scientific experiment that he had been planning for some time. He wanted to prove that lightning was indeed electricity.

He made a kite tied with two strings, one of silk and one of hemp. The silk string was for him to hold, while the hemp string would hold a better electrical charge. He also had a metal key, which he tied to the hemp string, and a Leyden jar, which is an instrument that can store an electrical charge. His son William was there to help him since he was more adept at kite flying.

They waited as the kite soared in the air. Just when they were about to call it quits, Franklin suddenly noticed that the loose threads of the hemp string were getting stiff and erect. He moved his finger near the key, and he felt an electrical spark.

The kite was never actually struck by lightning; if that had happened, Franklin likely would have been electrocuted, even though he took precautions to stay somewhat safe. Instead, the kite collected the ambient electrical charge from the wet atmosphere. The hemp string got wet in the rain and became a conductor, and the electrical charge was passed on to the key.

It is also important to note that Benjamin Franklin did not discover electricity during this experiment; electricity had already been discovered. Franklin also did not discover that lightning was electricity, although he thought he had. The same experiment had already been carried out in France a month prior. Still, Franklin's theory and experiment are the most well known, and he did demonstrate the connection between lightning and electricity. Franklin also invented the lightning rod, which was eventually used to protect tall buildings from lightning strikes.

Oxygen

Joseph Priestley was an Englishman who lived from 1733 to 1804. He was the first person to discover oxygen and describe some of its remarkable properties. Priestley discovered over a dozen other gasses as well. He also invented carbonated water and the rubber eraser. But his unorthodox religious writings and his unflinching support for the American and French Revolutions upset others. A crowd destroyed his home and his scientific equipment. He was hounded out of his town, and he eventually migrated to the United States, where he lived until his death.

But before all that happened, Priestley found that air was not an elementary substance but a mixture of many gases. In 1774, he conducted his most famous experiment using a twelve-inch-wide magnifying glass, focusing sunlight on a piece of reddish mercuric oxide to heat it and capture the emitted gas. He found that this gas caused a flame to burn intensely and kept a mouse alive about four times as long as a similar quantity of normal air. He called this gas "dephlogisticated air," which was later named oxygen by the French chemist Antoine Lavoisier.

Priestley later inhaled the gas himself and reported that he felt light and relaxed. He realized oxygen's medical and recreational use and wrote that this "luxury" gas had been inhaled by himself and two mice with none suffering any ill effects.

Of course, oxygen had important medical applications, and its discovery led to the development of new technologies, such as the oxyacetylene torch, which would change the metal-welding industry forever.

The Marine Chronometer and the Sextant

Mariners going on a long voyage needed to determine their position on the sea where no land was in sight. For this, it was necessary to know the latitude and longitude to accurately know their position on the map. Up until the middle of the 18th century, mariners were unable to determine their position at sea with accuracy, and they faced huge risks, such as shipwrecks or not reaching their destination before running out of supplies.

Navigators could determine their latitude by measuring the sun's angle at noon or by measuring the angle of Polaris or the North Star (in the Northern Hemisphere) at night. This was done by using a sextant, an instrument that could provide latitude while at sea. Of course, sailors had problems when the skies were cloudy.

Although various forms of sextants were used, British inventor and mathematician John Hadley perfected a sextant that could provide very accurate measurements in 1731. His sextant was used by mariners to find latitude at sea.

However, until the mid-1750s, accurate navigation at sea was an unsolved problem due to the difficulty in calculating longitude. To know the longitude, it is necessary to know what time it was where a ship currently was and what time it was at the port they had initially sailed from. Comparing local time with the time back home would tell the sailors how far around the earth they were from their home port. And if they knew the longitude of the port city where they started their journey, then they could more easily find the longitude of their current location.

The obvious solution to this problem was to get an accurate clock and set it to the time of their home port before setting sail. But until 1735, no accurate clock existed that could be relied upon at sea.

In 1714, the British government offered a prize of £20,000 to build a marine clock that could find the longitude at sea within half a degree. This meant the clock would be accurate to within 2.8 seconds, an accuracy that was considered unthinkable at that time.

Self-taught English inventor John Harrison took up the challenge and built various models of a clock, one of which was demonstrated to be sufficiently accurate to win the prize. The last watch made by Harrison in 1770 was even more accurate, allowing mariners to know their position very accurately wherever they were at sea.

Hot Air Balloon

Humans have always wanted to fly in the air like a bird. Two French brothers, Joseph-Michel and Jacques-Étienne Montgolfier, were prosperous paper manufacturers who were also interested in scientific experimentation. They were fascinated with the idea of seeing a balloon made of lightweight paper filled with heated air rise in the air.

The Montgolfiers built a balloon made of silk and lined it with paper that was thirty-three feet in diameter. They launched it in a crowded marketplace in Annonay, France, on June 4th, 1783. Nobody was on board. The balloon rose to over five thousand feet and stayed aloft for ten minutes, traveling more than a mile. This experiment encouraged the brothers, and they constructed a balloon about thirty feet in diameter made of taffeta and coated it with a varnish of alum for fireproofing.

King Louis XVI of France was invited to attend the demonstration. The king was so excited about the experiment that he wanted to test it for human flight by putting prisoners in a basket hung below the balloon. However, the Montgolfiers loaded the basket with a sheep, a duck, and a rooster. The experiment was successful, and the balloon flew for eight minutes and a distance of two miles, with all the passengers surviving the flight. This experiment was witnessed by the French king, Marie Antoinette, and a crowd of 130,000.

On October 15th, 1783, a balloon with a tether carried Jean-François Pilâtre de Rozier, a science teacher. The balloon soared over Paris for almost four minutes. And finally, on November 21st, Pilâtre de Rozier and a military officer made the first free flight in a hot air balloon. The pair flew from Paris, going about 5.5 miles in 25 minutes.

This was the start of human flight and ushered in a new era of human transportation. Today, hot air balloons are not used for human transportation on a large scale, but they are routinely used in scientific investigations of the atmosphere.

The Modern Thermometer

Several people attempted to perfect various types of thermometers, such as the water thermoscope by Galileo Galilei in 1593 and the air thermoscope by Santorio Santorio in 1612. However, neither Galileo's nor Santorio's instruments were very accurate.

The first modern mercury thermometer with a standardized scale was invented by Daniel Gabriel Fahrenheit in 1714. Fahrenheit used the first standard temperature scale for his thermometer. He divided the freezing and boiling points of water into 180 degrees. The number 212 was chosen as the boiling point, and 32 was chosen as the freezing point of water. This produced a scale that would not fall below zero, even when measuring the lowest possible temperatures that he could produce in his laboratory. This thermometer was very accurate.

The Celsius temperature scale is called the "centigrade scale." It was invented by Swedish astronomer Anders Celsius in 1742. Zero was the boiling point, and one hundred was the freezing point of water. The scale was divided into one hundred degrees. Later, a Frenchman named Jean Pierre Cristin inverted the Celsius scale, with zero as the freezing and one hundred as the boiling point of water. In 1948, by an international agreement, the Celsius scale was adopted as the standard international temperature scale, and it is the most widely used temperature scale today.

The Spinning Jenny and the Flying Shuttle

For a long time, the spinning of cotton into threads for weaving into cloth was a small cottage industry. The process was slow and labor-intensive. In 1764 or 1765, James Hargreaves, an English carpenter and weaver, worked on a new design of a cotton thread spinning machine.

Although he was illiterate, he understood the slow, laborious process of spinning thread. He also knew there was a shortage of sufficient thread for weavers. So, Hargreaves developed a machine that would increase the output of thread by increasing the number of spindles able to be operated by a single wheel.

A spinning jenny was a metallic frame with eight wooden spindles at one end. Eight rovings were attached to a beam on the frame. When extended, they passed through two horizontal bars. The worker would move these bars along the top of the frame, and the thread would be moved. At the same time, the spinner would turn a wheel. The spindles turned, and the thread was spun and wound onto a spindle.

Hargreaves kept the machine secret for some time, but cloth workers found out about this new labor-saving device that might threaten their jobs. They attacked his house and destroyed his machine. But Hargreaves was not deterred and continued the development and production of the machine.

In the first design, eight spindles were built into the machine, which spun the thread by turning a single wheel. This meant the operator could spin eight threads at a time just by moving a single wheel. The number of spindles was increased to 90 and then up to 120 in the newer designs, which resulted in a massive increase in the production of cotton thread.

Previously, in 1733, John Kay invented the flying shuttle, which was used in cloth weaving machines. In older loom designs, the shuttle was pushed through the threads by hand. If a wider size cloth was required, then two workers were needed to operate the loom.

Kay redesigned the loom and put the shuttle on wheels that ran on a track. The weavers used flat paddles to move the shuttle from one side to the other by pulling a cord. By using this method, one weaver could create fabrics of a larger width more quickly than before, improving the speed and quantity of the cloth.

The flying shuttle and the spinning jenny revolutionized the textile industry since a large quantity of cloth could be produced efficiently at a lower cost.

The Flush Toilet

In medieval England, people used "potties" and would simply throw the contents through a door or window into the street. The more affluent would use a "garderobe," a room with an opening suspended over a moat where waste could be dumped.

Common people relieved themselves in communal toilets at the end of the street. A huge public toilet was constructed in London that emptied directly into the River Thames. It caused massive pollution, which resulted in widespread stench and inflicted various types of diseases on the city's population.

In 1592, Sir John Harrington, a godson of Elizabeth I, was believed to have invented a toilet with a raised water reservoir connected to a pipe by which the water could flush the waste. This invention was ignored for almost two hundred years. In 1775, Alexander Cummings, a watchmaker, developed the S-shaped pipe under the toilet basin to keep out foul odors from the toilet room. This partly solved the problem of bad odors in the houses. However, sewage was still spilled into the streets, polluting the nearby rivers.

In 1858, when rotting sewage surrounded the city of London, creating a very bad stench, the government commissioned the building of a sewer system in London. The construction was completed in 1865. This resulted in a drop in deaths from cholera, typhoid, and other waterborne diseases.

Scientific Establishments

These scientific discoveries and inventions were mostly made by individuals, not groups or institutions. During the pre-Enlightenment era, new scientific establishments and associations were created for like-minded individuals to talk about ideas. The two most prominent were the Royal Society in England and the Académie des Sciences in France.

Although both institutions were founded in the 17th century during the Scientific Revolution, they continued to flourish, bringing together leading scientific minds during the Enlightenment for practical and philosophical discussions.

These establishments aided in promoting scientific exploration and nurturing a culture of scientific experimentation, research, and scholarship. They also helped disseminate scientific knowledge and encourage literacy, which, in turn, created a new breed of scientists.

Chapter 4 – Ambitious Lust for Absolute Power

There are many fables and myths associated with Catherine the Great of Russia. One gruesome tale suggests that Catherine perished while engaging in carnal activities with a stallion that went berserk and collapsed on her, causing fatal injuries. However, there is no evidence to validate this account. Most historians presume that it was likely fabricated by Catherine's adversaries to defame her and tarnish her reputation.

In truth, Catherine the Great passed away in her chamber at the Winter Palace in St. Petersburg on November 17th, 1796, at the age of sixty-seven. The reason for her demise was a stroke, which she had encountered several days earlier. Catherine the Great was one of the most triumphant and influential enlightened monarchs of the 18th century. But she was far from being the only one.

Enlightened Autocracy

Enlightened autocracy was a method of administration that emerged in Europe during the 18th century. It sought to unite the principles of autocracy, where a sovereign had complete power over their kingdom and people, with the ideas of the Enlightenment, which underlined rationality and the pursuit of knowledge.

Enlightenment thinkers believed their sovereigns should be enlightened, erudite individuals who utilized their power to bring about societal, economic, and political changes. They saw sovereigns as the ultimate authority and believed they had a responsibility to govern in the best interests of their subjects rather than simply maintain their power and privilege.

The significance of enlightened autocracy lay in the fact that it symbolized a new way of thinking about governance. Rather than regarding power as the only thing that mattered, the enlightened autocrats perceived it as a means to improve society. By embracing rationality and the pursuit of knowledge, sovereigns could (hypothetically) create a more equitable and fair society. The needs of the people would be taken into consideration, and the sovereign would be answerable to their subjects.

Enlightened despots proclaimed that their royal power emanated not from the divine right to rule but from a social contract that entrusted them with the power to govern. These despots believed the people could not improve their lives on their own and that it was their responsibility to help them. In many cases, these rulers were benevolent and did many good things, but in the end, they increased their hold over the masses and their authority. This self-serving philosophy stated that the sovereign knew the interests of his or her subjects better than they did. And if the monarch took responsibility for their subjects, then their subjects would have no need to engage in politics.

Enlightened autocracy emerged as a response to the challenges encountered by European monarchies after the Enlightenment became more popular. As mentioned before, the Enlightenment challenged many of the conventional sources of authority, including the right of kings and the authority of the Catholic Church.

Thus, some sovereigns believed that embracing the ideals of the Enlightenment would allow them to reinforce their power. They believed that by becoming enlightened, they could promote the well-being of their subjects and cement their place in history as "enlightened rulers."

Enlightened sovereigns, such as Frederick II of Prussia, encouraged economic and social reforms, including the eradication of serfdom and the promotion of education. Catherine the Great of Russia and other rulers fostered cultural and intellectual developments, sponsoring the arts and science and advocating the ideals of the Enlightenment.

Enlightened despots recognized the significance of education, both for themselves and for their people. They believed that an educated populace could better contribute to society and support the monarch's objectives. Many enlightened despots supported schools and promoted education.

Although enlightened despotism achieved some success in advocating reforms and enhancing the living standards of the subjects, it had its limitations. Firstly, enlightened despots retained absolute authority, which meant they could suppress dissent and restrict political freedoms. Additionally, many of the implemented reforms were still restricted in scope and did not address the fundamental inequalities prevalent in European societies.

Overall, enlightened despotism represented a crucial moment in European history, highlighting the tension between conventional sources of authority and the Enlightenment's ideals. Although it had its limitations, it demonstrated the possibility of using power for the greater good and advocated the notion that governments had a duty to promote their citizens' welfare. The legacy of enlightened autocracy can still be observed today, especially in the belief that governments work for the greater good and aid the people under their rule.

Frederick the Great of Prussia

A portrait of Frederick the Great.
https://en.wikipedia.org/wiki/File:Friedrich_II.,_K%C3%B6nig_von_Preu%C3%9Fen_(Frisch).jpg

Frederick the Great of Prussia (also known as Frederick II) is widely regarded as one of the most prosperous and influential enlightened monarchs of the 18th century. During his long reign from 1740 to 1786, he implemented significant reforms that helped transform Prussia into a modern, affluent, and powerful state.

Frederick made some progress in improving the conditions of his subjects. For example, he was quite successful in controlling grain prices. The government storehouses would store sufficient amounts of grain and distribute it in times of need to the people so they could survive hard times when the harvest was poor. Frederick was also a good administrator, and he improved the bureaucracy and civil service. He abolished torture, granted amnesty to political prisoners, and established an independent judiciary, which ensured fair and impartial justice.

Frederick was in favor of freedom of thought. He was also quite tolerant in religious matters, with the people being allowed to follow their religious beliefs and practices, not a state-mandated religion. Frederick was largely non-practicing, although Protestantism became the favored religion. While he protected and encouraged trade by Jewish citizens of the empire, he repeatedly expressed strong anti-Semitic sentiments. Still, he expanded the Jewish population's rights, allowing them to settle in Prussian territories and practice their religion freely. Before this, they had been largely persecuted. Frederick also encouraged immigrants of various nationalities and faiths to come to Prussia.

Moreover, he promoted education, particularly in the sciences, and encouraged cultural and artistic growth. He was a prolific writer and composer, and his court attracted many of the leading intellectuals of the era.

Frederick implemented major economic reforms. He encouraged trade and commerce, promoted agricultural productivity, and supported industry growth. He abolished serfdom and other feudal obligations, granting greater freedom to the peasantry and the middle class. He also reformed the tax system, making it more equitable and efficient, and established a centralized bureaucracy, which consolidated his power and promoted effective governance.

However, despite Frederick's numerous successes, he was not without failures and controversies. He participated in numerous wars during his reign, often to expand Prussian territory and influence, which resulted in a significant loss of life and resources. He also faced criticism for his authoritarianism, which was deemed incompatible with his professed commitment to Enlightenment values. He censored the press, restricted freedom of speech, and suppressed dissent.

Frederick the Great of Prussia was a complex and multifaceted figure. As an enlightened monarch, he embraced many of the Enlightenment's values, promoting religious tolerance, economic advancement, and cultural and intellectual growth. However, his authoritarian tendencies and military ambitions attracted significant criticism, highlighting the tensions inherent in the concept of enlightened despotism.

Charles III of Spain

A painting of Charles III.
https://en.wikipedia.org/wiki/File:Charles_III_of_Spain_high_resolution.jpg

Charles III of Spain reigned from 1759 to 1788. He was probably the most successful European ruler of his time. He provided firm, consistent, intelligent leadership. He chose capable ministers, and his personal life was rather chaste and nondramatic, which won him the respect of the people.

During his reign, he transformed Spain into a more contemporary state. His policies sought to promote economic growth and social justice. Charles deregulated the economy, established chambers of commerce, set up new industries, and promoted science.

In Madrid, Charles established a new customs house, hospital, porcelain factory, and museum of nature. He also oversaw improvements to the sewage system, street lighting, and roads. The municipal government was reorganized, and theaters were renovated.

Charles III was a patron of the arts and science. He stimulated the growth of the arts, endorsing artists and musicians and promoting the development of Spanish literature and theater. It seems as if no aspect of public life was immune from the new spirit of progress.

King Charles III implemented significant agrarian and industrial reforms aimed at enhancing productivity and advocating economic growth. He stimulated the growth of commerce and trade, eliminating trade barriers and promoting free trade within Spain and with other European countries. Reforms included a royal decree "ennobling" the mechanical trades. He established government factories, providing productive employment for the poor.

However, his reforms did not always work as planned. "Ennobling" the mechanical trades did not produce the desired results. However, the economy did experience an upturn. The population of Spain increased from eight million to twelve million under his rule, leading to an increased demand for food and a sharp rise in prices. The larger population benefited the large landowners in the south and the small farmers near growing towns, such as Barcelona. The most remarkable feature of this economic revival was the emergence of a modern cotton textile industry in Catalonia.

The obsolete iron industry in the Basque region started to slowly modernize. The fishing industry grew in Galicia, where the Catalan immigrant fishermen became quite prosperous. Catalonia also became a hub for the brandy trade.

There were also many reforms in the financial sector, with the abolition of many duties and taxes, the encouragement of local markets, and the opening of trade with America.

However, Charles III was not without his failures. His efforts to encourage economic growth often came at the expense of the lower classes, and his policies regarding the working classes were often severe and exploitative. He implemented significant tax reforms that disproportionately affected the poor, and his labor policies were frequently oppressive and restrictive. His legacy as an enlightened monarch persists in Spain, but his reign also reminds us of the contradictory nature of enlightened absolutism.

Catherine the Great of Russia

A portrait of Catherine the Great.
https://en.wikipedia.org/wiki/File:Catherine_II_by_J.B.Lampi_(1794,_Hermitage).jpg

The reign of Catherine the Great of Russia lasted from 1762 to 1796 and was marked by significant innovations and reforms that transformed Russia into a major power on the world stage.

Catherine's ascendancy to power in a coup d'état was a theatrical and violent event in Russian history. In 1762, Catherine's husband, Peter III, became the tsar of Russia. Peter was an unpopular and peculiar ruler who had little interest in governing. He could barely even speak Russian, as he had been raised in what is today Germany. He was more engrossed in military affairs and was known to admire the Prussian king, Frederick the Great, to the extent of garbing himself in Prussian military uniforms.

Catherine, on the contrary, was popular with the Russian populace and had a strong interest in politics and culture. She had been brought to Russia from her native Germany as a teenager to wed Peter, but their union was unhappy and fraught with tension.

After only a few months on the throne, Peter's erratic behavior and unpopular policies estranged many of his supporters. On June 28th, 1762, Catherine and her supporters staged a coup d'état. The coup was swift. Peter was arrested and forced to abdicate in favor of Catherine. He was later killed under mysterious circumstances, with many believing that he was assassinated on Catherine's orders.

One of Catherine's greatest achievements as an enlightened monarch was her advocacy of education, culture, and the arts. She established schools, hospitals, and orphanages, and she championed the growth of the arts and science. She was a prolific writer and corresponded with many of the leading intellectuals of the day. She also patronized the construction of the Hermitage Museum, which became home to one of the largest and most prestigious art collections in the world.

Another one of Catherine's accomplishments was the expansion of the Russian Empire. She annexed Crimea, the Caucasus, and portions of Poland, significantly broadening Russia's borders and influence. This expansion helped to establish Russia as a major European power and laid the groundwork for its subsequent domination in the 19th century.

Nonetheless, despite her many achievements, Catherine still faced controversies. Her greatest failure was perhaps her incapability to address the fundamental issues confronting Russia's social and economic systems. She maintained serfdom, a feudal system of labor that kept millions of peasants in bondage, and failed to implement significant reforms to the country's political and economic structures. This failure led to widespread social unrest and opposition, which contributed to the eventual downfall of the Romanov dynasty.

An example of Catherine the Great's ruthlessness was her response to Pugachev's rebellion, which took place from 1773 to 1775. She ordered a brutal crackdown on the rebels, using military force to suppress the rebellion. Thousands of rebels were captured, and Pugachev was eventually captured and executed. His body was dismembered in Moscow. Catherine's retribution was severe, with widespread executions, torture, and reprisals against those believed to have supported the rebellion. Tens of thousands of people were killed during the suppression of the Pugachev Rebellion.

Catherine's enlightened rhetoric was often at odds with her actual policies and practices. She was an autocratic ruler who limited the people's freedom of the press, speech, and assembly. She also engaged in imperialistic wars, and her policies toward Poland and other territories were often merciless and exploitative.

Catherine died in 1796 in St. Petersburg, Russia. Her death marked the conclusion of a long and eventful reign that spanned over three decades and had seen significant political, social, and cultural changes in Russia.

Catherine the Great's reign was marked by achievements and progress in many areas, but it was also marred by instances of brutality, oppression, and criticism. Nevertheless, Catherine's impact on Russian history and her contributions to the country's political and cultural development cannot be denied. She remains a significant figure in Russian and world history.

Leopold I of Tuscany

Leopold I of Tuscany, also known as Grand Duke Leopold I, was one of the most prosperous and forward-thinking enlightened monarchs of the 18th century. Throughout his reign, from 1765 to 1790, he enforced noteworthy reforms that aimed to modernize Tuscany into a more effective and fair state.

One of Leopold I's accomplishments as an enlightened monarch was the introduction of significant agricultural and industrial reforms aimed at enhancing efficiency and stimulating fiscal growth. He encouraged commerce and trade by abolishing trade obstacles and promoting free trade. Leopold also instituted the first modern insurance system in Europe, safeguarding people against loss or destruction of property.

Leopold I was a sponsor of the arts and sciences. He supported the Accademia dei Georgofili, which concentrated on the study of agriculture, and also promoted the Accademia delle Belle Arti, which focused on the arts. Leopold encouraged the proliferation of the arts, sponsoring artists and musicians, and endorsed the development of Tuscan literature and theater.

Leopold abolished capital punishment and ensured smallpox vaccinations were easily obtainable for everyone. He created hospitals for the mentally ill, becoming one of the first to do so. Although these hospitals were not like the ones we have today, his doctors did not believe in torturing or punishing those who lived there.

But of course, Leopold I had his faults. And those faults mainly came to light when Leopold took over the Holy Roman Empire from his brother, becoming Leopold II. Although he continued some of his enlightened policies while ruling this vast territory, he also used brute force. He didn't want to be unpopular with his subjects, mainly the nobles. To put down a disturbance, Leopold placed thousands of people who had been freed from serfdom back under the yoke. Leopold was a politician, and he played the politician's game when his hand was forced.

Leopold I's reign helped to transform Tuscany into a more contemporary and prosperous state. But his policies, especially once he became the Holy Roman emperor, could be unjust.

Joseph II of Austria

Joseph II, also known as Joseph the Reformer or Joseph the Great, was a Holy Roman emperor and archduke of Austria who ruled from 1765 to 1790. Joseph was Leopold I's brother. Joseph was a proponent of enlightened absolutism. He is known for his ambitious and wide-ranging reforms aimed at modernizing Austria and improving the lives of his subjects. However, his reign was also marked by controversy, challenges, and, ultimately, an unfinished legacy.

One of Joseph's greatest accomplishments was his policy of religious toleration. He ended the Catholic Church's control over education, allowing for greater intellectual freedom and the proliferation of scientific inquiry. He also granted religious protections to Protestant and Orthodox minorities and promoted the rights of Jews. Additionally, he reformed the judicial system, granting greater protections to defendants and enhancing the efficiency of legal proceedings.

Joseph also reformed the economy and the social system. He implemented significant agrarian and industrial reforms that were aimed at increasing productivity and economic growth. One of his major acts was abolishing serfdom, granting greater liberties to the peasantry and the bourgeoisie. He restructured the taxation system and eliminated trade barriers, encouraging greater economic integration within the Holy Roman Empire and beyond.

However, Joseph's enlightened policies were often met with substantial opposition. His efforts to centralize power and eliminate regional autonomy were met with resistance from the aristocracy, who witnessed their traditional privileges and powers being affected by what they saw as radical moves. His attempts to reform the Catholic Church also encountered substantial opposition from conservative clergymen, who saw their influence and power being eroded. Moreover, his policies toward Hungarians and other ethnic minorities were frequently heavy-handed and contributed to nationalist sentiment and opposition.

Another captivating aspect of Joseph's life was his relationship with his mother, Empress Maria Theresa. The two were notoriously close, with Joseph serving as his mother's right-hand man and chief advisor for many years. Nonetheless, their relationship was not without its strains and conflicts, primarily over Joseph's progressive policies and his desire to modernize the empire.

Joseph II was a controversial figure whose reign was marked by both successes and failures. His promotion of religious tolerance and social modernization helped to transform the Holy Roman Empire into a more efficient and fair state, but his efforts to centralize power and eliminate regional autonomy often encountered resentment from the elite and the Hungarians, making him unpopular and isolating him politically from other nations. His legacy as an enlightened monarch remains a topic of discussion by historians today.

Absolute Rulers: Flourishing or Failures?

Absolute rulers were commonly regarded as the ultimate power in their territories, as their authority was not subject to any constraints. This could be both an asset and a flaw. On the one hand, absolute rulers had the power to make sweeping transformations and enact policies they believed were in the best interest of their subjects. However, this also meant they could act with impunity and frequently had little thought for the wishes of their subjects.

The absolute rulers mentioned in this chapter were powerful in their own right, and their reigns had an enduring impact on their individual nations and European history. While they were all absolute rulers, they also espoused the principles of the Enlightenment and sought to foster progress and reform, reflecting the evolving attitudes of the period.

Nonetheless, these rulers were just that, rulers. They wanted to retain their power and ensure that power would be passed down to their heirs. Numerous people chafed under their rule and resented the fact they had no voice in governance. In addition, the concentration of authority in the hands of a solitary ruler frequently resulted in corruption, nepotism, and abuses of power. This, in turn, weakened the legitimacy of the monarchy and led to rebellion or revolution.

All in all, the triumph and acceptance of absolute monarchs varied extensively. While some were able to employ their power to foster progress and ease the lives of their subjects, others were regarded as oppressive and corrupt, leading to widespread discontent and even revolution.

Chapter 5 – Core Pillars of Enlightened Thought

The core pillars of Enlightened thought are reason, individualism, skepticism, and progress. Other crucial concepts include the separation of church and state and constitutional governance.

Reason

The pre-Enlightenment era spans a lengthy period of history, but one of the earliest intellectuals who championed the use of reason was the ancient Greek philosopher Aristotle (384-322 BCE). Aristotle believed that reason was the key to comprehending the world and that humans could utilize it to ascertain truth and knowledge. He emphasized the significance of observation, analysis, and logic.

Aristotle's ideas about reason influenced many subsequent thinkers, including the medieval philosopher Thomas Aquinas (1225-1274), who endeavored to reconcile Aristotle's philosophy with Christian theology. Aquinas contended that people could employ reason to understand the natural world but that faith was essential to comprehend spiritual matters.

Accepting reason was a radical departure from how people contemplated understanding. Before the Enlightenment, knowledge was frequently based on teachings from authority figures, such as the church or the government. The reason was a lack of education, books, and other reliable sources of information. However, Enlightenment thinkers repudiated authority figures being used as sources of knowledge, arguing they were frequently dogmatic and superstitious, basing information on arbitrary rules instead of reason.

One of the most eminent and influential figures associated with the rise of reason to comprehend knowledge was French philosopher René Descartes, who lived between 1596 and 1650. Descartes argued that people could acquire knowledge through reason and that skepticism was crucial for testing the validity of claims.

Of course, there were opponents to the rise of reason, primarily the Catholic Church. The church saw the emphasis on reason and empirical evidence as a menace to its authority, so it actively opposed many ideas and practices associated with the Enlightenment. For instance, the church condemned Galileo for his endorsement of the heliocentric model of the solar system, which contradicted church teachings.

Some Enlightenment intellectuals were also critical of rationality and stressed the limitations of reason. The German philosopher Immanuel Kant contended that reason had its restrictions. In his opinion, there were certain aspects of the world, such as morality and the existence of God, that could not be comprehended through reason alone.

The achievement of the scientific method, the uptick of new forms of communication, the evolution of new philosophical and political ideas, and the application of reason to daily life persuaded individuals of the significance of logical thinking.

Individualism

The emergence of individualism symbolized a significant shift in reasoning about the individual's role in society, highlighting the significance of personal rights and self-rule. The idea of individualism profoundly affected the progress of modern liberal democracy and the preservation of individual rights and freedoms.

But what exactly is individualism? Simply put, individualism promotes the idea that the individual is more important than the state. Enlightenment thinkers who touted this belief wanted people to realize they had goals and dreams that deserved to be fulfilled, not shoved to the side so the government could force them to work in the fields.

One of the critical factors that contributed to the rise of individualism during the Enlightenment was new economic and social systems, such as the rise of trade, the ascension of the middle class, and the decline of feudalism. These changes created new opportunities for social mobility and economic prosperity.

Enlightenment thinkers were pivotal in promoting individualism, asserting that individuals should be free to pursue their interests and desires without interference from the state or other authorities. They stressed the importance of the right to free expression, religious freedom, and the right to possess property. They also attempted to limit the power of the state and other establishments to safeguard these rights.

One of the most influential intellectuals associated with the rise of individualism during the Enlightenment was English thinker John Locke, who lived between 1632 and 1704. Locke stated that individuals were endowed with fundamental rights and that the state should preserve these rights. He also contended that governments should derive their authority from the consent of the governed.

Another advocate of individualism was French philosopher Jean-Jacques Rousseau, who lived from 1712 to 1778. He claimed that individuals were born free and equal and entitled to certain natural rights, including the right to life and liberty. He stressed the importance of individual self-rule and self-determination, contending that individuals should be able to pursue their interests and desires without undue interference from the state or other forms of authority.

Rousseau's ideas significantly differed from traditional forms of social organization, highlighting the importance of duty, obligation, and deference to authority. His emphasis on individualism paved the way for a new understanding of the relationship between individuals and society.

Paradoxically, Rousseau, while himself a supporter of individualism, also criticized certain aspects of individualism that he saw as contributing to social inequality and injustice. Rousseau argued that individualism could lead to self-centeredness and social fragmentation. He believed it could undermine the social bonds and shared values necessary for a cohesive and just society.

Other adversaries of individualism included religious authorities and conservative political leaders who viewed individualism as threatening the traditional forms of power and the social hierarchy. They argued that individualism could lead to moral decadence, social disorder, and political instability, so they sought to promote more conventional forms of social organization and authority.

Individualism is a prominent belief today, with many countries, including the United States, South Africa, and Germany, basing their government on it. Individualism will likely continue to spread in the years to come.

Skepticism

Skepticism pertains to a discerning mindset toward conventional beliefs and practices. Enlightenment thinkers moved away from the idea of traditional authority and sought to challenge established norms and conventions. They believed in the importance of questioning information and validating ideas through empirical observation and scientific inquiry instead of being handed information from a clergyman or king. Skepticism goes hand in hand with reason, as skeptics wanted to use logic to prove old beliefs as being wrong.

One of the most significant proponents of skepticism was the French philosopher René Descartes. Descartes stressed the significance of doubt as a means of challenging accepted beliefs and assumptions. He argued that individuals should rely on their own thoughts and judgments to evaluate the veracity of various claims.

Scottish thinker David Hume, who lived between 1711 and 1776, is widely regarded as one of the greatest champions of skepticism. He argued that knowledge could only be derived from sense and experience. Hume stated that any claims that could not be verified through observation and experimentation should be treated with skepticism. In his opinion, people's knowledge of cause-and-effect relationships is based on a constant conjunction of events rather than any logical connection between them.

Hume also applied his skeptical approach to religious and ethical claims, arguing that these could not be established through reason or observation and were therefore based on faith and sentiment. Hume's skeptical views on religion and morality were contentious. They attracted widespread criticism but also contributed to a broader cultural shift toward a more critical and scientific approach to social and moral issues.

Religious institutions and figures often denounced skeptics, mainly regarding religious claims, arguing that faith was indispensable for establishing the truth of religious doctrines. Some philosophers and intellectuals were also critical of skepticism, arguing that it led to relativism or nihilism, which undermined the foundations of knowledge and morality.

German philosopher Friedrich Nietzsche criticized this skeptical approach to knowledge, arguing that it eroded the possibility of objective truth and left individuals without any moral or intellectual compass.

Nietzsche's critique of skepticism was part of a broader cultural shift toward a more subjective and existentialist approach to knowledge and truth, which rejected the notion of objective reality in favor of a more subjective and individualistic worldview. This concept is a little complex, but to put it simply, Nietzsche believed that people viewed the world based on their own experiences and that there was no one "right" way to live.

The impact of religious and political upheavals prompted many individuals to scrutinize the authority and claims of leaders. For example, the Protestant Reformation challenged the power of the Catholic Church, encouraging individuals to read and interpret the Bible for themselves, contributing to a more critical approach to religious claims.

Similarly, the political revolutions of the time, such as the American and French Revolutions, challenged the authority of traditional monarchies and aristocracies and encouraged individuals to question the legitimacy of political power.

Progress

Enlightenment thinkers believed that society could improve through reason and the application of scientific knowledge, a concept known as progress. Progress was a significant shift in how people viewed human history and society. Before the Enlightenment, people believed that the world was static and unchanging and that human history was merely a cycle of rises and falls.

Enlightenment thinkers challenged this view, arguing that society progressed and improved through reason, skepticism, and individualism. Many Enlightenment thinkers believed that progress was essential for humans to flourish and create a just society. Enlightenment thinkers produced works on topics like science, philosophy, economics, and politics, using rhetoric to persuade their readers of the importance of progress.

Some Enlightenment philosophers, such as Immanuel Kant, contended that progress resulted from man's search for logic. Others, such as Adam Smith, regarded progress as the outcome of the growth of commerce and trade, which facilitated the creation of wealth and the spread of ideas.

French philosopher and author Voltaire was one of the most influential figures in shaping the notion of progress. He was a prolific writer who created works on various topics, including history, politics, philosophy, and religion. He was a staunch advocate of reason and individualism, believing that progress was critical for human prosperity and creating a fair society.

In his celebrated work *Candide*, Voltaire ridiculed the idea that everything was for the best in this "best of all possible worlds," arguing instead that the world was full of suffering and injustice that could only be overcome through the pursuit of enlightened values. He championed religious tolerance, free speech, and the separation of church and state, all of which he believed were essential for creating a more open-minded society.

One of the key drivers of progress during the Enlightenment was the rise of science, which allowed people to understand the natural world better and develop new technologies and innovations. This, in turn, led to improvements in medicine, agriculture, transportation, and other fields, which helped to better people's lives.

The Romantic poets and thinkers who emerged in the late 18th and early 19th centuries rejected the emphasis on reason and praised emotion, imagination, and intuition instead. They were suspicious that human progress could be achieved by applying reason and technology. They criticized the Enlightenment's faith in progress as a naive and dangerous idea. They thought science, technology, and an emphasis on logic would make life dull and devoid of creativity and romance.

German philosopher Friedrich Nietzsche argued that the emphasis on reason and progress led to a loss of meaning and purpose in modern life. He advocated rejecting Enlightenment values in favor of a more individualistic and life-affirming philosophy.

The rise of progress during the Enlightenment was the product of a complex interplay of social and political factors, and it was propelled by a growing sense of optimism and a belief in the power of human reason to shape the world for the better.

The Separation of Church and State

The separation of church and state refers to the notion that the government should not be involved in ecclesiastical matters and vice versa. Individuals should also be able to practice their own religion or lack thereof of their own volition.

The idea of the separation of church and state originated as a reaction to centuries of religious strife and persecution in Europe. The idea that religion and government should be kept apart was considered a way to foster tolerance and prevent the abuses of authority that had been pervasive throughout much of European history.

The French philosopher Voltaire argued that religious leaders should have no say in government affairs. He believed that the government should be indifferent to religious matters, allowing individuals to practice whatever religion they choose without fear of retribution.

English philosopher John Locke maintained that the government should be restricted in its power and allow individuals to have the liberty to pursue their own religious convictions. Locke considered religious tolerance to be crucial in promoting social harmony and thought that the government had no right to meddle in religious belief or practice.

In the United States, the separation of church and state was formalized in the First Amendment to the Constitution, which states, "Congress shall make no law respecting an establishment of religion, or prohibiting the free exercise thereof." This principle has been a cornerstone of American democracy ever since and has helped to ensure that the government does not exhibit partiality toward any religion or use its power to suppress religious minorities.

However, some disagreed with the concept. French philosopher Jean-Jacques Rousseau opined that religion and the state should be intertwined. He argued that religious convictions and practices were indispensable for creating a sense of community and social cohesion. He also held that the state had a duty to safeguard and advance religious values.

Rousseau's views on the relationship between religion and the state directly opposed the separation of church and state. Nevertheless, his opinions ultimately did not triumph, and the principle of the separation of church and state remains a crucial tenet of contemporary Western democracies.

Constitutional Government

A constitutional government refers to a government where power is limited by a written constitution that delineates the rights and responsibilities of citizens and the government's powers. Enlightenment intellectuals held that a constitutional government was essential for safeguarding individual liberties and preventing the abuse of power by those in authority.

The Enlightenment was a period of immense political upheaval, and many intellectuals grappled with questions of how to create a just and stable society. One of the principal ideas that emerged during this time was constitutional government.

The growth in demand for constitutional governments was closely connected to the social contract theory, which held that a government should be founded on a mutual agreement between the people and their rulers. This theory emphasized the significance of individualism and the need to restrict the government's power to safeguard the rights of citizens.

One of the most influential advocates of a constitutional government was the English philosopher John Locke, who contended that government should be founded by the consent of the governed and that a constitution should restrict authority figures.

Another prominent champion of constitutional government was French philosopher Montesquieu, who lived from 1689 to 1755. In his notable work *The Spirit of Law*, published in 1748, Montesquieu advocated for the separation of powers in government and the limitation of any individual or faction holding all the power. He believed that the best form of government combined elements of a monarchy and democracy. Montesquieu also thought a constitution was mandatory to protect individual rights and hinder abuses of power.

The rise of constitutional governments was closely linked to the growth of capitalism and commerce. As trade expanded, individuals began to demand greater safeguards for their property rights and individual liberties, which led to the establishment of constitutions and other legal protections.

Several monarchs and aristocrats of the time opposed restricting their power through a constitution. Some conservative thinkers, such as Edmund Burke, argued that society's traditions and customs should lay the groundwork for a government rather than abstract principles or documents like a constitution. Burke also feared that excessive change or reform could lead to confusion and instability. He saw the importance of religious institutions for the moral stability and good of the state. He argued that the French Revolution would end disastrously because its foundations ignored human nature's and society's complexities.

The American and French Revolutions present examples of effective constitutional governments in action, which helped to spread the idea.

However, the French Revolution was much bloodier and unfair, as many elites were persecuted and killed during the Reign of Terror. Ultimately, the democratic government of France fell to Napoleon Bonaparte, who created an empire that was seen as more liberal, although his power was still absolute.

The rise of the printing press and the wider availability of books and pamphlets enabled all of these Enlightenment ideas to reach a vaster audience. The essential pillars of enlightened thought stress the significance of rationality, individualism, progress, and skepticism in promoting a better understanding of the world and society.

Chapter 6 – Intellectual Titans Who Changed the Course of History

Imagine a time when the world was still in the grip of superstition, religious dogma, and monarchial rule. A time when knowledge was the privilege of the elite and dissent was met with brutal punishment. Against this backdrop, a group of radical thinkers emerged whose ideas would change the course of history forever.

From daring explorers to brilliant philosophers, from visionary economists to revolutionary writers, these great men were not content to sit back and accept how things were. They were driven by a fierce desire to understand the world around them and to make it a better place.

In the following short biographies, you will observe these extraordinary men's thrilling lives and ideas and understand their impact on their world and ours.

John Locke

A portrait of John Locke, one of the most influential Enlightenment thinkers.
https://commons.wikimedia.org/wiki/File:John_Locke.jpg

John Locke (1632-1704) was an English philosopher and physician who is considered one of the most influential figures of the Enlightenment. He is known for his contributions to political philosophy, the theory of knowledge (epistemology), and educational theory.

As a young man, Locke was determined to pursue his dreams, despite the many obstacles in his path. He struggled to make ends meet and was constantly battling illness, but his passion for knowledge and his unrelenting spirit drove him forward. Locke's most remarkable feat was his ability to rise above the limitations imposed on him by society, despite being born into a time when social class and birthright dictated one's destiny.

Locke's father and mother came from Puritan trading families, with clothiers on his father's side and tanners on his mother's. His father earned a living as an attorney and clerk to the Justices of the Peace in Somerset. He owned some land but not enough to enable his family to live as aristocrats. However, it was enough to lead a reasonable life.

Until his mid-thirties, Locke lived a rather unexciting life. For more than three decades, he was involved with politics, but in his late fifties, he became very famous as a philosopher. He published his writings, with one of his most notable works being *An Essay Concerning Human Understanding*, published in 1689.

The theory of knowledge set out in *An Essay Concerning Human Understanding* is, in some ways, extremely skeptical. He believed humans were born as blank slates that were filled with their own unique experiences in life. In other words, people were not born with innate ideas of how to live; that was something a person gained over time. He also stated that there was a limit to the knowledge a person could gain.

As he writes in his essay, "Knowledge, say you, is only the Perception of the Agreement or Disagreement of our own Ideas: but who knows what those Ideas may be?"

Locke also famously believed that governments should be based on the consent of the governed and that individuals have a right to life, liberty, and property. He argued that the government's role was to protect these rights. If a government failed to do so, then the people had the right to overthrow it.

His philosophy obviously had a significant impact on the development of modern democracy, and his ideas were influential in the American and French Revolutions. He also wrote extensively about education, advocating for an approach that emphasized individualism and encouraged students to think for themselves.

In the last decade and a half of Locke's life, as an old, sick, and immensely distinguished man, he was at last in a position to see the scale and meaning of his achievements. Locke was a man who refused to accept the status quo and instead chose to challenge it at every turn. His ideas continue to shape the world we live in today.

Baruch Spinoza

Baruch Spinoza (1632–1677) was a rebel in every sense of the word. As a child, he attended a Jewish school and the synagogue, where he studied Hebrew and the works of Jewish and Arabian theologians.

Although he was brought up in a strict Portuguese-Jewish family in Amsterdam, he challenged the traditional religious beliefs of his community and dared to think for himself. His unorthodox ideas about God and nature would eventually lead to his excommunication from the Jewish community.

Spinoza was branded a heretic and accused of trivializing God's role in the universe and human affairs. He was expelled from the Jewish community for speaking against religion and was declared a heretic. He disputed the existence of miracles and the afterlife and challenged the authority of the Bible. His book titled *Theologico-Political Treatise* was declared as an evil work inspired by the devil. His magnum opus, *Ethics*, put forward a system of breathtaking originality but was condemned by the Catholic Church. It was put on the list of banned books.

Undeterred, Spinoza continued to explore his radical philosophy, rejecting the notion of a personal God and embracing the power of reason to understand the natural world. He saw human emotions and passions as obstacles to rational inquiry and argued for a strong separation between church and state.

There is an interesting anecdote about Professor Albert Einstein, the author of the theory of relativity, who declared his belief in "Spinoza's God." In 1929, Einstein received a telegram from Rabbi Herbert S. Goldstein of the Institutional Synagogue in Germany, who asked Einstein, "Do you believe in God?" Einstein wrote back to the rabbi, "I believe in Spinoza's God, who reveals himself in the orderly harmony of what exists, not in a God who concerns himself with the fates and actions of human beings."

So, who was Spinoza's God that Einstein believed in? According to Spinoza, the church had fallen for the illusion of an anthropocentric God, an external being acting in the world of human affairs and intervening according to his whims. Spinoza claimed that the church made God similar to a king who grants rewards for submission and delivers punishments for any sins. It is interesting to note that famous philosophers, such as John Calvin and René Descartes, also used the metaphor of God being similar to a king in their writings.

Despite his radical ideas, Spinoza's works were widely read and respected during his lifetime, and he remains one of the most important figures of the Enlightenment. His works inspired other Enlightenment thinkers, including Voltaire, Kant, and Hume. His ideas were considered dangerous and revolutionary during his time, but his influence would be felt for centuries to come.

Montesquieu

Charles-Louis de Secondat, Baron de La Brède et de Montesquieu (1689-1755), was a prominent French philosopher and writer. Born to a noble family, Montesquieu quickly distinguished himself as a brilliant thinker and writer with a razor-sharp intellect and a deep passion for justice.

Montesquieu was primarily interested in politics and law. He was a proponent of a government with limited powers in which the leaders had to follow the law. Montesquieu believed the government's power should be separated into branches so that no single person or group held too much power. Montesquieu's ideas also included skepticism toward the rigid social structure of France. He was a vocal advocate for human rights, including the abolition of slavery, and his work helped to pave the way for the French Revolution and the rise of democracy across Europe.

Montesquieu's most famous work, *The Spirit of Laws*, published in 1748, was a groundbreaking contribution to political theory. In it, he argued that the best form of government was one that had a separation of powers with checks and balances. This idea would go on to become a cornerstone of modern democracy and constitutional governments.

In addition to his political philosophy, Montesquieu was a social commentator, and his writings often reflected his concerns about the state of French society. He was critical of the French monarchy, which he saw as oppressive and corrupt, and he championed the rights of individuals and the importance of personal freedom. His call for more rights was seen as dangerous by the ruling elite. His writings were often censored and suppressed.

Today, he is widely regarded as one of the greatest philosophers of the Enlightenment, and his contributions to political theory and social commentary continue to shape our understanding of the world around us.

Voltaire

A portrait of Voltaire.
Nicolas de Largillière, CC0, via Wikimedia Commons;
https://commons.wikimedia.org/wiki/File:Nicolas_de_Largilli%C3%A8re_-_Portrait_de_Voltaire_(1694-1778)_en_1718_-_P208_-_mus%C3%A9e_Carnavalet_-_5.jpg

Born François-Marie Arouet, Voltaire (1694-1778) was a French writer, historian, and philosopher who is considered one of the greatest literary figures of his time. His life was filled with dramatic events that shaped his beliefs and inspired his writing.

As a young man, Voltaire was known for his sharp wit and rebellious spirit. He was educated by Jesuits and studied law but quickly became disillusioned with the French legal system. He began writing satirical poems and plays that mocked the aristocracy and the church. As a result, he soon gained a reputation for being a troublemaker. He was frequently at odds with the authorities.

In 1717, Voltaire was arrested and imprisoned for insulting a nobleman. He continued to write and develop his philosophical ideas while in prison. About a year later, he was released, but he did not get to enjoy the sights of France for too long. In 1726, he was exiled to England, where he was exposed to the works of John Locke and other Enlightenment thinkers. He returned to France in 1729 and soon became embroiled in a series of controversies over his writings and beliefs.

Voltaire was a passionate advocate for human rights and religious tolerance, and his ideas had a profound influence on the development of modern Western thought. Part of his influence stems from the fact that he wrote far more than anyone else. The first-ever edition of his complete works, currently being undertaken by the Voltaire Foundation in Oxford, will result in some two hundred volumes!

Voltaire was a master of virtually all literary genres. His writings include poetry in many different styles, satire, plays, opera, history, short prose works, and even a scientific treatise. In addition to all that, he has the most extensive correspondence of any writer of the period.

Voltaire maintained a lifelong interest in science and philosophy, and he corresponded with some of the most influential thinkers of his time, including John Locke, Isaac Newton, and Jean-Jacques Rousseau. Voltaire's life was filled with drama, and his writing faced many controversies, but his legacy as a champion of reason, freedom, and justice continues to inspire people worldwide today.

David Hume

David Hume (1711-1776) was a Scottish philosopher, historian, and economist who played a key role in the Enlightenment. Hume's most important contributions to philosophy came in the form of his skepticism and belief in empiricism. He was skeptical of traditional metaphysical concepts, such as causality (the belief that one event causes another event to occur), and argued that people's knowledge of the world was based on sensory experience rather than abstract reasoning.

Hume grew up in a family of intellectuals and was driven by an insatiable curiosity about the world around him. As a young man, Hume studied law and even worked briefly as a merchant, but his true passion was philosophy. He spent countless hours reading and writing. In his groundbreaking work, *A Treatise of Human Nature*, Hume famously argued that there is no connection between cause and effect and that our beliefs about the world are based on habit and association rather than reason.

He proposed that traditional religious beliefs were outdated and needed to be replaced with a more scientific approach. He argued that reason and experience should be the foundation of all knowledge and that scientific inquiry should be used to understand the natural world. David Hume's philosophy is often represented as part of a movement that was started by John Locke in 1690. The main theme of this movement is that men have no knowledge of the world but what they derive from experiences, such as feelings, bodily sensations, sounds, smells, and tastes.

In addition to his philosophical work, Hume was an important historian and economist. His *The History of England* is still widely read today and is considered a classic. Regarding economics, Hume argued that a stable monetary system was essential for economic growth and that government intervention in the economy should be limited.

Jean-Jacques Rousseau

Jean-Jacques Rousseau (1712-1778) was born in Geneva, Switzerland. He was a larger-than-life figure whose ideas and writings shook the foundations of the Enlightenment. He rose to become one of the most celebrated thinkers of his time, despite facing constant adversity and personal turmoil.

Though Rousseau never received a formal education, he showed a prodigious intellect and a deep curiosity about the world around him at an early age. His studies in philosophy and literature led him to Paris in 1742, where he soon became the toast of the intellectual elite. He became a music teacher and befriended many of the leading academics of the day, including Denis Diderot and Voltaire. During this time, he began to write and publish his works, including his first essay, *A Discourse on the Moral Effects of the Arts and Sciences*, which won him widespread acclaim.

Rousseau entered an essay competition with a work entitled *Discourse on the Arts and Sciences*. His essay was in response to a question of whether progress in science and arts will improve or corrupt human morality or not. Guess who won the contest? Rousseau did, and it brought him greater recognition as a philosopher.

In his essay, Rousseau proposes that the sciences and art conflict with virtuousness and morality. He goes on to say that science often gives false information, which could be dangerous to society. When people study arts and science, they become lazy and scorn virtues. When people follow and indulge in art, people are rewarded based on their talent, which causes inequality in society. Enlightened values, if employed correctly, would make people wealthy, and in Rousseau's view, wealth destroys morality.

But Rousseau was not content to simply bask in his success over his essay, even though it was seen as controversial by many. Instead, he used his platform to challenge Enlightenment thoughts. He rejected the idea that reason was the sole path to truth and championed the importance of human emotion and intuition. He criticized the social and political structures of his time, arguing they were built on a foundation of oppression and injustice.

Despite the acclaim that his ideas received, Rousseau was constantly beset by personal problems. His relationship with his mistress, Thérèse Levasseur, was tumultuous at best, and his feelings of isolation and disillusionment seeped into his writing.

As the years went on, Rousseau's ideas became more radical and confrontational. His masterpiece, *The Social Contract*, laid out a vision for a just society, calling for the government's power to be derived from the people themselves and for individual freedom to be balanced against social responsibility.

Like any other Enlightenment thinker, Rousseau's ideas were not without critics, and he soon found himself at the center of controversy. His writings were accused of being anti-Christian, and his ideas were seen as a threat to the established order. He never went to jail, avoiding it by going into self-imposed exile in England.

Rousseau was known for his idealistic views on society and his belief in the natural goodness of man. He was also known for his rather eccentric behavior and had a reputation for being paranoid and a hypochondriac. Today, Jean-Jacques Rousseau remains one of the most enigmatic and captivating figures of the Enlightenment.

Denis Diderot

Denis Diderot (1713-1784) was a bold and courageous French philosopher and writer who fearlessly challenged traditional authorities and advocated for greater freedom of thought.

Diderot was deeply influenced by Enlightenment ideas. He believed that knowledge should be accessible to everyone, not just the educated elite. In 1745, he was introduced to Jean le Rond d'Alembert, a mathematician and philosopher who shared his views. Together, they began work on the *Encyclopédie*.

The *Encyclopédie* was a massive undertaking, requiring the collaboration of hundreds of contributors. It aimed to collect and organize knowledge on a wide range of subjects, including science, philosophy, art, and politics. Diderot served as the editor. He oversaw the project and wrote many of the articles himself.

Diderot was a prolific writer. He wrote plays, novels, and essays on many subjects. His most famous novel, *Jacques the Fatalist and His Master*, is a satirical work that challenges traditional notions of fate and free will.

In *Jacques the Fatalist*, a master and his servant ride through France, with the servant appearing to be free and master of his own will. The pair travel across the country, with the story revealing a panoramic view of 18th-century society. But while the servant seems to choose his own path, he remains convinced of one philosophical belief: that every decision he makes, however whimsical, is wholly predetermined.

Diderot's novel is playful and comic. It is also a compelling exploration of Enlightenment philosophy. Brilliantly original in style, it is considered to be one of the greatest novels of post-modern literature.

Diderot's work was often controversial and led to frequent censorship and persecution by the authorities. To avoid trouble, Diderot published his books anonymously. Soon after the *Pensées philosophiques* appeared in 1746, it was publicly burned in July of that same year. By 1749, the authorities confirmed that he was the author of these dangerous books. After the publication of *Lettre sur les aveugles*, he was jailed in the Dungeon of Vincennes for three months.

In *Lettre sur les aveugles*, Diderot argued that a blind man who could suddenly see would not understand what he was looking at. He has to perceive things to understand them. Diderot extended this argument to the spiritual realm, saying that if a person has to perceive things to understand them, then there is no universal spiritual truth.

Nevertheless, after Diderot's release from prison, he continued to write and challenge traditional ideas, helping shape the intellectual and cultural life of France.

Adam Smith

An etching of Adam Smith.
https://en.wikipedia.org/wiki/File:AdamSmith.jpg

Adam Smith (1723-1790) was a Scottish philosopher and economist who is widely regarded as the father of modern economics. From a young age, Smith was fascinated by the world around him, and he immersed himself in his studies. He devoured the works of the great thinkers of his time, such as David Hume.

Smith became interested in the ideas of free trade and the division of labor. He believed that a free market would lead to the greatest economic growth.

However, it was Smith's groundbreaking work, *The Wealth of Nations*, that made him a legend in the annals of economic thought. This monumental work, published in 1776, laid out Smith's vision of a free-market economy, one in which individuals were free to pursue their own self-interests without interference from the state. It outlined his ideas about the government's role in economic affairs and argued that government intervention in the market should be limited. Smith's ideas had a significant impact on the development of economics and political philosophy, and his legacy continues to influence economic thought today.

Smith was also a significant figure in moral philosophy. He believed that moral behavior was rooted in sympathy and empathy for others and that individuals had an innate sense of justice and morality that should guide their actions.

Immanuel Kant

An engraving of Immanuel Kant.
https://commons.wikimedia.org/wiki/File:Immanuel_Kant_3.jpg

Immanuel Kant (1724-1804) was a German philosopher whose life was defined by his unwavering dedication to reason, truth, and intellectual rigor. Kant grew up in a world that was rapidly changing, both politically and culturally. Despite the challenges of his time, Kant was a man of singular focus and determination. He studied philosophy, mathematics, and physics at the University of Königsberg and soon developed a reputation for his brilliance and original thinking.

As Kant embarked on his career as a philosopher, he was driven by a burning desire to uncover the fundamental truths of existence. He spent long hours in his study, poring over texts and working through complex problems, always striving to arrive at a deeper understanding of the world around him.

Kant's work was groundbreaking, as he challenged long-held assumptions about the nature of reality. His major works, including the *Critique of Pure Reason* and the *Critique of Practical Reason*, were among the most important philosophical texts of his time.

In *Critique of Pure Reason*, published in 1781, Kant seeks to reconcile rationalism and empiricism by examining the nature and limits of human knowledge. Kant distinguishes between *phenomena* (appearances) and *noumena* (things as they are), stating that our knowledge is limited to the realm of *phenomena*. He introduces the concept of transcendental idealism, suggesting that our perceptions are shaped by innate categories that structure our experience of the world. Kant also discusses the limitations of reason and contradictions that arise when reason tries to go beyond the limits of experience.

The *Critique of Practical Reason*, which was published in 1788, focuses on ethics and moral philosophy. In this book, Kant shifts his focus from theoretical reason to practical reason, specifically exploring the nature of morality and the foundations of ethical decision-making. Kant insists that practical reason, or the ability to make moral judgments and to act accordingly, is fundamental to human freedom. He introduces the concept of the categorical imperative, a moral principle that requires individuals to act according to maxims that can be universally applied without contradiction.

Kant lived a modest and frugal lifestyle, and his income primarily came from his work as a professor at the University of Königsberg, where he taught for most of his career. Although Kant was widely respected as a philosopher, and his works gained significant recognition, he did not accumulate a significant amount of wealth. Kant's focus was primarily on his intellectual pursuits and philosophical writings rather than financial gain.

Kant left behind a legacy that has continued to inspire and influence generations of thinkers and scholars. His ideas about reason, ethics, and human nature remain as relevant today as they were during his lifetime, and his contributions to philosophy and history will continue to be celebrated for centuries to come.

Cesare Beccaria

A portrait of Cesare Beccaria.
https://en.wikipedia.org/wiki/File:Cesare_Beccaria.jpg

Cesare Beccaria (1738-1794) was born in Milan, Italy, and became a man of fierce intellect and unwavering moral courage.

As a young man, Beccaria was interested in the ideas of the Enlightenment, which emphasized the importance of reason and liberty. He immersed himself in the study of philosophy, economics, and law. He also studied the works of the great thinkers of his time, such as Voltaire and Montesquieu.

His book, *On Crimes and Punishments*, challenged many of the traditional assumptions of criminal justice, arguing that punishments should be designed to deter crime rather than to exact revenge. Beccaria also believed the legal system should be based on the principles of equality and fairness.

These were radical ideas and put Beccaria at odds with the powerful institutions of his time. But he was undaunted by the challenge, and he poured his heart and soul into his work, spending years meticulously researching and writing his masterpiece.

In the end, Beccaria's efforts paid off. His book became one of the most influential books of his time, helping to shape the modern world as we know it today. And though Beccaria himself is long gone, his legacy lives on, inspiring generations of thinkers and scholars to push the boundaries of what is possible and explore the limits of human knowledge.

The Legacy of Great Men

The great men of the Enlightenment were pioneers who challenged the conventional wisdom of their time and ushered in a new era. Their ideas have left an indelible mark on our world and continue to inspire and guide us today.

Their contributions to philosophy, science, economics, literature, and politics continue to influence our understanding of the world. By embracing critical thinking, freedom of speech, and the value of the individual, these remarkable men laid the foundation for the modern world we inhabit.

As we reflect on the impact of these great men, we are reminded of the power of human intellect, perseverance, and courage. Their stories and ideas should inspire us to push the boundaries of knowledge, stand up for what is right, and strive for a better world. The great men of the Enlightenment remind us that progress is possible and that even in the face of adversity, we have the power to shape the future.

Chapter 7 – Women Who Defied the Limits of Their Time

Although Rousseau was a great intellectual and popular thinker of his day, he famously said that women were naturally inferior to men in terms of intellectual capacity and were better suited for domestic tasks and familial roles.

During the Enlightenment, there was a group of brilliant women whose ideas and writings challenged the traditional gender roles that had been firmly entrenched in society for centuries. Despite facing numerous obstacles and constraints, these women defied social norms and expectations. Many of their names have been lost in the pages of history, but we do know of several women whose contributions to the advancement of society and the pursuit of knowledge are undeniable.

Damaris Masham

Damaris Masham (1658-1708) was an English philosopher and writer who engaged in philosophical debates with some of the leading thinkers of her time, including John Locke. She was born into a prominent family and received a thorough education in languages, literature, and philosophy.

Little is known about her education, but she did have the advantage of being born into a family with a large library and a father who was one of the most learned men of his generation. She learned French, as was deemed requisite for a gentlewoman of the time, and she taught herself Latin.

Lady Masham wrote two books, *A Discourse Concerning the Love of God* (1696) and *Occasional Thoughts in Reference to a Vertuous or Christian Life* (1705), which were printed anonymously. Both books address philosophical issues that were topical at the time, such as love and moral virtue. Lady Masham believed that human beings are rational, social animals and are motivated by the pursuit of happiness.

She insisted on the importance of revelation and faith and denied that religion based purely on reason was possible. However, she also thought that religious belief that ignores the role of reason creates superstition. As she states, "An irrational religion can never rationally be conceived to come from God."

Lady Masham was particularly interested in John Locke's writings and corresponded with him extensively on topics ranging from politics to the nature of the soul. Her correspondence with Locke helped to shape his ideas and, in turn, influenced the development of philosophy during the Enlightenment. Lady Masham's writings on philosophy and religion were highly regarded in the 18th century, although they have received less attention in modern times.

Mary Astell

Mary Astell (1666-1731) was an English writer and philosopher. She is best known for her advocacy for women's education and her contributions to feminist theory. She can be called one of the earliest English feminists.

Astell began her writing career as a playwright. She later turned her attention to philosophy and wrote several influential works on education and equality. Her two books, *A Serious Proposal to the Ladies* (with part one coming out in 1694 and part two in 1697) and *Some Reflections upon Marriage* (1700), made her quite famous.

The first book, *A Serious Proposal to the Ladies*, is an appeal for more education for women. She urged women to do their best to gain knowledge and develop their own minds and the ability to think for themselves, all of which would guide them in living virtuous lives.

Astell had a problem with the cultural assumptions about femininity and the popular attitude about women. According to most people (women included), women did not demonstrate the same kind of intellectual ability as men because women were inherently more closely united to their bodies. Astell was worried that women were not being prepared for real-world issues and societal problems. Instead, women were being taught trivial things, such as social skills to look feminine and be nice and proper wives to their husbands. The average woman was not given an education that allowed them to develop their reasoning skills.

To overcome this, Astell proposed self-discipline and the establishment of an academy along Platonist lines, a place where women could receive proper education in religion and philosophy.

In her second book, *Some Reflections upon Marriage*, she examines women's subordination in marriage and their lack of freedom. She asked women not to marry and make promises to serve men or take vows of obedience. She considered these kinds of marriages as slavery and wanted women to choose husbands who would treat them as equals.

In her early twenties, Astell rejected a marriage proposal from a man who did not share her interests. She felt he would stifle her intellectual growth. She decided to remain single and devote herself to her writing.

Astell's ideas were radical at the time, and she faced much criticism and opposition from those who believed that women should be confined to domestic roles. However, her work inspired later feminist movements, and she has been recognized as an important contributor to the Enlightenment's legacy of advancing individual rights and freedoms.

Émilie du Châtelet

Émilie du Châtelet (1706-1749) was a French mathematician and writer who is best known for her translation and commentary of Isaac Newton's *Principia Mathematica*. She was born into a wealthy aristocratic family and received a thorough education in languages, literature, and mathematics. She married the Marquis de Châtelet, but their marriage was not a happy one, as they lived separate lives. However, she took on many lovers. One of her most prominent lovers was none other than Voltaire, who she met in 1733. He not only became her lover but also her companion and mentor.

Du Châtelet was keenly interested in the natural sciences, especially the writings of Newton, Gottfried Leibniz (a German mathematician who developed the binary system), and Christian Wolff (a German philosopher). Her advanced knowledge in physics and mathematics allowed her insight into Newton's physics that other women would not have. She helped shift France away from Cartesian physics, which was mostly conjecture drawn up by Descartes, toward Newtonian physics. Du Châtelet was also a scientist in her own right, searching for a metaphysical basis for Newtonian physics.

She set out to translate Newton's *Principia* into French, a project that took her several years to complete. Along the way, she added her own commentary and insights to the work, which helped to clarify and expand on Newton's ideas. Du Châtelet's translation and commentary helped to popularize Newtonian physics in France and beyond and had a lasting impact on the development of science during the Enlightenment.

In 1737, du Châtelet entered a competition to explain the nature of fire. She conducted experiments to disprove that fire was something material. Voltaire was also doing similar yet separate experiments to arrive at the same conclusion. Both of them published their results, and they both won prizes, along with another scientist, Leonhard Euler, who took the first prize.

Emilie du Châtelet died in childbirth at the age of forty-two in 1748. Her newborn daughter died around twenty minutes later. Her contributions to physics, mathematics, and philosophy during the Enlightenment, as well as her advocacy for women's rights, cannot be overstated. Her work has inspired generations of scholars, particularly women working in science and mathematics.

Laura Bassi

Laura Bassi (1711-1778) was an Italian physicist who became the first woman to earn a university chair in a scientific field, which was an extraordinary achievement for that time.

Bassi was the daughter of Giuseppe Bassi, a successful liberal lawyer. Bassi was an extremely precocious child. She received an excellent private education at home in very difficult subjects, such as mathematics, Latin, metaphysics, and philosophy.

In 1732, Bassi was invited by the University of Bologna to be appointed as a full professor of natural philosophy. Her incredible academic record and competence were so stellar that it did not matter that she was a woman.

About six years later, Bassi married Giovanni Giuseppe Veratti, a physician and fellow professor. The pair became a power couple in scientific circles. Bassi continued her work in physics, with a particular interest in Isaac Newton's theories of classical mechanics. Although she wrote around thirty papers, only four were ever printed.

Laura Bassi paved the way for future generations of women to enter academia. She also made significant contributions to the field of physics and advocated for women's rights and education.

Olympe de Gouges

Olympe de Gouges (1748-1793) was a French writer and activist. She is best known for her feminist writings and her advocacy for women's rights.

De Gouges began her writing career as a playwright. Her most famous work, *The Declaration of the Rights of Woman and the Female Citizen*, was published in 1791 as a response to the French Revolution's Declaration of the Rights of Man and of the Citizen, which excluded women. In her book, de Gouges writes, "Woman has the right to mount the scaffold; she must equally have the right to mount the rostrum."

De Gouges argued that women were equal to men and should have the same rights and opportunities. She advocated for women's access to education, property, and the right to vote. She also wrote about other social issues, pushing the boundaries of what was considered acceptable in public discourse.

She was not a philosopher, but she was known for her morally astute analysis of women's role in society, for her reimagining of the intersection of gender and political engagement, for her conception of civic virtue and her pacifist stance, and for her advocacy of selfhood for women, people of color, and children. She was among the first to demand the emancipation of slaves. She wrote about the rights women deserved, including those who had been divorced or were unwed mothers, and the protection of orphans, the poor, the unemployed, the aged, and illegitimate children.

De Gouges's ideas were ahead of her time, and she faced criticism and persecution for her views. Although de Gouges's ideas were not widely accepted in her lifetime, her work inspired later feminist movements. She challenged the prevailing social and political norms of her age and advocated for equality and justice for all individuals.

De Gouges was aware of the dangers of speaking out against the government, but she refused to remain silent. She wrote a letter to the revolutionary leader Maximilien Robespierre in which she criticized the violence and bloodshed of the Reign of Terror and called for an end to the executions. Despite the risks involved, de Gouges continued to speak out against the government and was eventually arrested and charged with treason. She was executed by guillotine.

Mary Wollstonecraft

Mary Wollstonecraft (1759-1797) was an English advocate for women's rights during a time when women were often relegated to the margins of society. Her writings challenged the status quo and laid the groundwork for a new era of feminist thought and activism.

Wollstonecraft began her writing career as a translator and journalist. She later turned her attention to philosophy and wrote several influential works on women's education and equality. Her most famous work, *A Vindication of the Rights of Woman*, was published in 1792 and argued for equal rights.

In her book, Wollstonecraft fearlessly argued that women were just as capable as men and deserved the same educational opportunities and political rights. Her words were a call to arms for women everywhere, inspiring them to demand their rightful place in society and fight for equality.

Wollstonecraft argued that women were not naturally inferior to men but were held back by their lack of education and opportunities. She called for the establishment of educational institutions for women and argued that women should have access to the same intellectual and political freedoms as men.

She goes on to say, "I shall first consider women in the grand light of human creatures, who, in common with men, are placed on this earth to unfold their faculties." She also insisted that it is essential for women's self-respect that they should have a right to earn and support themselves.

The book had a significant impact on the development of feminist theory and the broader social and political movements of the time. Her writings helped to inspire generations of women to fight for their rights and paved the way for the feminist movements of the 19th and 20th centuries.

In addition to her work on women's rights, Wollstonecraft was also an advocate for social justice and democratic reform. She believed in the importance of individual freedom and human rights, arguing that government should be structured to promote the common good rather than serve the interests of the ruling class.

One of the most dramatic moments in Wollstonecraft's life came when she traveled to France during the French Revolution. While there, she witnessed the tumultuous events that were occurring and became involved in radical political circles. She fell in love with an American diplomat named Gilbert Imlay. She met Imlay while living in Paris, and the two began a tumultuous relationship. Although they had a child together, Imlay proved to be unfaithful, and their relationship eventually collapsed. In a state of despair, Wollstonecraft attempted to take her own life by jumping into the Thames in London. She was rescued by a passerby and survived the ordeal.

Wollstonecraft's suicide attempt was a critical moment in her life, but it also speaks to the challenges she faced as a woman during the Enlightenment. Women of her time were often denied access to education and opportunities, and their personal lives were constrained by social expectations. Wollstonecraft's struggle to find meaning in her life serves as a reminder of the ongoing struggle for gender equality and the importance of fighting for human rights.

Mary Wollstonecraft's legacy continues to be recognized and celebrated today. Her contributions to feminism, literature, philosophy, and social reform have had a profound impact, and her ideas continue to inspire and shape modern discourse on gender equality, human rights, and social justice. Her work continues to be studied, debated, and celebrated by scholars, activists, and individuals who seek to promote equality and social change.

Sophie Germain

Sophie Germain (1776-1831) was a French mathematician who made important contributions to number theory and mathematical physics. Germain was born into a wealthy family and showed an early aptitude for mathematics. However, as a woman, she was initially excluded from formal education. Undeterred, she taught herself mathematics and began corresponding with leading mathematicians of her time.

Her breakthrough came when she discovered a way to model the vibrations of elastic surfaces, which helped to explain the phenomenon of musical acoustics. Germain went on to make significant contributions to number theory, including her work on Fermat's Last Theorem, which had remained unsolved for centuries. Despite facing discrimination due to her gender, Germain persisted in her work and was eventually recognized as a pioneer in her field.

Criticism Against These Women

Enlightenment male thinkers held a range of views on women and their role in society. However, many of these views were shaped by deeply ingrained patriarchal beliefs that saw women as inferior to men and relegated them to subordinate roles in the home and family.

One notable example of this perspective can be found in the works of Jean-Jacques Rousseau. In his work *Emile, or Treatise on Education*, Rousseau argues that women's natural inclination is to be domestic and nurturing and that they are best suited to the role of wife and mother. According to Rousseau, women's education should be focused primarily on developing their moral and emotional qualities rather than on acquiring knowledge or skills that would allow them to participate more fully in society. And Rousseau was not the only Enlightenment thinker who felt this way.

It is indeed amazing that these women went against the grain by challenging traditional gender roles and expectations, asserting their right to participate in intellectual and political spheres. These female thinkers changed the prevailing ideas of their time and helped to lay the groundwork for a more just society through their work. Their determination, courage, and brilliance helped them to leave a lasting legacy for future generations of women to build upon.

Chapter 8 – The American Enlightenment

It should not be surprising to hear that the American Enlightenment was highly influenced by the European Enlightenment. In the 18th century, colonists in the Thirteen Colonies realized their voice wasn't being heard in British Parliament. As time wore on, they realized they wanted something more than "tyranny." They wanted independence. They wanted a democracy.

Famous American Enlightenment Thinkers

But who led the charge? Who came up with the ideas of a self-representative government and the rights to life, liberty, and the pursuit of happiness? Let's take a look at some of the most influential American thinkers during this time.

Benjamin Franklin (1706-1790)

A portrait of Benjamin Franklin.
https://en.wikipedia.org/wiki/File:Joseph_Siffrein_Duplessis_-_Benjamin_Franklin_-_Google_Art_Project.jpg

Almost everyone knows the name Benjamin Franklin. He was an American scientist, inventor, and statesman. His experiments with electricity helped to further science during the Enlightenment. He also invented the bifocals and the Franklin stove, which was designed to produce more heat and less smoke.

Franklin played a pivotal role outside of the realm of science. He helped draft the US Constitution and created many civic organizations, including the first fire department in Philadelphia. Although he initially owned slaves, he later argued for abolition and sought to integrate African Americans into society.

Franklin served as an ambassador to France, and he also dealt with the British Parliament when he tried to get it to repeal the Stamp Act. Franklin has rightfully been called "the most accomplished American of his age." He believed in practical knowledge and the application of reason in everyday life, and thus, his writings and inventions reflected his Enlightenment ideals.

John Adams (1735-1826)

Another Founding Father of America was John Adams. He was known for his defense of individual rights, his advocacy of republicanism,

Before becoming a leader of the American Revolution, Adams was a lawyer who emphasized a person's right to counsel and the idea that one was innocent until proven guilty. He even defended British soldiers involved in the Boston massacre, successfully winning his case. Adams was against the Stamp Act and was also against insurrection, at least at first. As tensions grew, his opinions changed, especially when the British government wanted to pay the governor of Massachusetts instead of the colony's legislature, putting the governor deeper into the Crown's pocket.

Adams did not actively serve in the war, instead serving as a diplomat in Europe, where he sought to secure support for the war effort. He became the first vice president and the second president of the United States. He lost his reelection for another term to the presidency, partly due to accusations of becoming too despotic, as he had passed laws that restricted immigration and criminalized those who wrote negative statements about the government.

Nevertheless, Adams is remembered as an Enlightenment thinker, and it is worth noting that out of the first twelve presidents, Adams and his son were the only ones who never owned slaves. He once famously said, "I have, through my whole life, held the practice of slavery in such abhorrence, that I have never owned a negro or any other slaves, though I have lived for many years...when the practice was not disgraceful...and when it has cost me thousands of dollars for the labor and subsistence of free men."

Thomas Paine (1737-1809)

Unlike Franklin and Adams, Thomas Paine was not born in the colonies. He was born in England, moving to the colonies in 1774, just in time for the American Revolution. Paine was a political activist, philosopher, and writer, and he is best known for his influential works, *Common Sense* and *The Rights of Man*.

Common Sense, published in 1776, promoted the idea of American independence from Britain. The pamphlet became the best-selling work in America, even hundreds of years later. *The Rights of Man* defends the French Revolution, saying that a revolution should happen when a government does not support the rights of the people.

Paine promoted democratic principles, individual rights, and the need for social and political reform. His writings advocated for the overthrow of the monarchy and the establishment of democratic governments, which greatly influenced the American Revolution.

Thomas Jefferson (1743-1826)

An iconic portrait of Thomas Jefferson.
https://en.wikipedia.org/wiki/File:Thomas_Jefferson_by_Rembrandt_Peale,_1800.jpg

Thomas Jefferson is another one of those household names in America, mainly because of his work on the Declaration of

Independence. Jefferson wrote many other works in which he emphasized the importance of individual liberty, religious freedom, and democratic ideals.

But let's dive into his most influential work: the Declaration of Independence. Although Jefferson was the original author of it, it was edited by the Second Continental Congress, so not all of his initial ideas made it to the final draft. For instance, Jefferson included a passage about how King George III had forced slavery on the colonies. "He has waged cruel war against human nature itself, violating its most sacred rights of life and liberty in the persons of a distant people who never offended him." The Second Continental Congress was worried Jefferson's article (which was much longer than that quote) would upset the Southern colonies, which greatly depended on slave labor. They wanted the Declaration of Independence to pass, not stall over something that even people in the North were not willing to fully give up yet.

Thomas Jefferson had a complicated relationship with slavery. He famously owned slaves, but he also believed the practice was evil. Regardless of his stance on abolition, his ideas on governance and human rights, as expressed in the Declaration of Independence, reflected Enlightenment principles and continue to influence American political thought.

James Madison (1751-1836)

James Madison is often referred to as the "Father of the Constitution," as he played a key role in drafting the US Constitution, primarily the Bill of Rights, which protects individual liberties such as freedom of speech, religion, and the press. He helped organize the Constitutional Convention, which helped bring about the revolutionary document in the first place.

Madison studied political philosophy at school, becoming entrenched in the ideas of the Enlightenment. Like the other American Enlightenment thinkers, he was outraged over the Stamp Act. Although Madison served in the American Revolution, his poor health made him sit out most of the battles. However, he was amazing with a pen, helping to create the Federalist Papers and the Bill of Rights, among many other essays and pamphlets. The Bill of Rights guarantees certain freedoms and ensures the separation of power, which are undeniably Enlightenment ideals. The First Amendment is like something pulled out of a European Enlightenment book: "Congress shall make no law respecting an establishment of religion, or prohibiting the free exercise thereof; or abridging the freedom of speech, or of the press; or the right of the people peaceably to assemble, and to petition the Government for a redress of grievances."

There were so many other American Enlightenment thinkers and Founding Fathers who had a lasting impact on American society and government, such as Ethan Allen and Alexander Hamilton. They influenced the ideals and principles that shaped the American Revolution, the formation of the United States as a democratic republic, and the drafting of key documents, such as the Declaration of Independence and the US Constitution. Their emphasis on reason, individual rights, religious tolerance, and the pursuit of progress continues to be reflected in American political thought and the country's democratic governance to this day.

John Locke and His Impact on the American Revolution

American Enlightenment thinkers were greatly inspired by the thinkers who had come before, with John Locke perhaps being one of the most influential. Locke's political philosophy emphasized the fundamental rights of individuals and the social contract between citizens and government.

Locke's ideas were especially important when it came time to draft the Declaration of Independence. The Declaration of Independence's statement that all individuals possess certain unalienable rights, including life, liberty, and the pursuit of happiness, was a statement made by Loke, except Jefferson adjusted his statement slightly, replacing "property" with "happiness." Locke's ideas about limited governance and the necessity for citizens to have a voice in decisions affecting their lives played a role in shaping the United States Constitution.

In France, whose revolution we will briefly cover in the next chapter, Locke's ideas were embraced by the masses who desired to challenge the power of the monarchy and the aristocracy. Locke's emphasis on individual rights and the social contract provided a framework for the French demands of liberty, equality, and fraternity.

The Declaration of the Rights of Man and of the Citizen, another declaration partly inspired by Locke's philosophy, affirmed that all citizens are born free and equal and possess certain unalienable rights, including ownership of property, freedom of speech, and religion.

Social Contract Theory and the Concept of Natural Law

The social contract theory and the notion of natural law are two Enlightenment concepts that had a substantial impact on political and social thought. The social contract theory suggests that individuals should come to an agreement to establish governance and maintain social order.

According to this theory, individuals consent to relinquish some of their individual freedoms in exchange for security and protection, which would be provided by the government. The theory of a social contract is based on the belief that individuals have innate rights that are inviolable.

Similarly, the concept of natural law asserts that ethical and moral principles are innate in nature and apply to all human beings, irrespective of culture, society, or tradition. These principles are deemed self-evident and provide a foundation for developing fair social and political systems.

Both the social contract theory and natural law were pivotal ideas during the American Enlightenment, as well as the European Enlightenment. These concepts provided a framework for revolutionary thoughts and played a significant role in developing democratic governance and modern legal systems. Today, the principles of the social contract theory and natural law continue to spark debates about individual entitlements, social justice, and the role of governance in society.

But how did the American Enlightenment go from being thoughts inked on paper to actions that caused a revolution? What was the trigger? Well, there were quite a few, but one of the most well known was the idea that Britain should not tax the colonies if the colonists had no representation. "No taxation without representation" became a rallying cry against the unjust Stamp Tax, which was one of the major catalysts for the American Revolution.

The Stamp Tax

In 1765, British Parliament issued the Stamp Tax. The Stamp Tax required all colonial printers to pay a tax to the British on any paper used in printing in the colonies, including items like playing cards. As a receipt, an embossed revenue stamp was to be fixed on the document.

Colonists considered the tax to be illegal because they had no voice in Parliament, which means the law passed without them having any input on it. Protests were held throughout the colonies, threatening tax collectors with violence. The British Parliament finally backed off and repealed the Stamp Act in March of 1766, but the colonial reaction set the stage for the American independence movement.

As time passed, more unjust acts were passed, including the Townshend Acts and the Tea Act. Bostonians rebelled against the Tea Act by staging the Boston Tea Party, where they dumped over three hundred chests of tea into the harbor. The British government was outraged and passed the Intolerable Acts in 1774, which the colonists heavily resisted. That September, they formed the First Continental Congress, which drafted a measure outlining the colonists' grievances and called for a boycott of British goods. The members of the First Continental Congress also wrote a letter to the king, asking him to repeal the Intolerable Acts.

When the king didn't respond, and after hostilities broke out when British forces attempted to take stockpiled weapons and gunpowder from the colonists, the Second Continental Congress was formed. The American Revolution had begun, and the Second Continental Congress got to work on drafting a constitution.

The actions men and women took varied depending on the person. The more fervent revolutionaries, such as the Patriots, were not afraid to advocate violence and protests early on. Others preferred a more conservative route, such as drafting pamphlets and petitioning Parliament. History tends to focus on the men during this period, but women played an important role as well. For instance, the Daughters of Liberty was created in 1765. These women boycotted British goods, instead making their own goods at home. Many textiles were imported from Britain, and the Daughters of Liberty put on public demonstrations where they spun their own clothing, bringing awareness to other women and men that the colonies could survive without British goods.

We won't dive into the battles of the American Revolution in this book, but suffice it to say the colonists won. They successfully set up a democratic form of government, with three separate branches of government and a constitution that is still in use today. The colonists demonstrated to the world that it was possible to achieve liberty and personal freedoms. Of course, those freedoms didn't extend to everyone at the time, and it took quite a while for the major European monarchies to fall or transform into more constitutional ones, but the American Revolution laid another stone on the path to progress.

The Six Great Ideas

With that timeline out of the way, let's look at six ideas that made up the core of American Enlightenment philosophy. Some of these ideas are similar to European Enlightenment ideals, but others are unique to the American colonies.

Republicanism

Republicanism was a political philosophy that emphasized the importance of civic virtue and the common good. It advocated for a system of government where citizens participated in public life, and the welfare of the nation was prioritized over personal interests. The American Enlightenment emphasized the idea of a virtuous citizenry that actively participated in the political process and promoted the well-being of the community.

Conservatism

Conservatism refers to a belief in the preservation of traditional institutions and values, including religion, the social hierarchy, and the monarchy. While this idea was not as dominant as other ideas, such as liberalism and republicanism, conservatism still played a vital role in shaping American society and politics during the American Enlightenment.

Deism

Deism was a religious and philosophical belief system that rejected traditional religious doctrine and advocated the use of logic to understand the natural world. Deists believed in a distant, impersonal God who created the universe but does not intervene in human affairs. They emphasized the importance of reason and rejected religious dogma, advocating for a more rational and scientific approach to understanding the world.

Toleration

Toleration was the idea of allowing religious and intellectual diversity and promoting religious freedom and freedom of thought. During the American Enlightenment, there was a growing emphasis on religious tolerance, with many thinkers arguing for the separation of church and state and the right to practice religion without fear of persecution. This idea of tolerance also extended to intellectual diversity, as Enlightenment thinkers believed in the importance of open discourse and the free exchange of ideas.

Liberalism

Liberalism, at least in the context of the American Enlightenment, referred to the belief in individual liberty, limited government, and the protection of natural rights. American liberals of this era were influenced by philosophers like John Locke. They believed that individuals had inherent rights, such as life, liberty, and property, and that the government existed to protect these rights. They championed the idea of a social contract between the people and the government, stating that the government should be accountable to the people and should be limited in its powers.

Scientific Progress

The American Enlightenment was marked by a strong emphasis on scientific progress and the application of reason and observation to understand the natural world. Enlightenment thinkers promoted the scientific method as a means of understanding and solving problems and saw science as a way to uncover the laws that governed the universe.

These Enlightenment beliefs contributed to the formation of the principles that shaped the American Revolution and the subsequent development of the United States as a democratic republic. The American Revolution inspired other groups of people to speak out against tyranny, most notably in France.

Chapter 9 – Quest for Liberty and Equality

"Égalité, liberté, fraternité" was the battle cry that reverberated through the boulevards of Paris. It seemed as though the people of France had reached the limit of their patience in the late 18th century. The mob took to the streets, armed with little more than their fierce courage and dogged determination, and began a quest for freedom that would change the course of history in France and the world.

In the summertime of 1789, the thoroughfares of Paris were like a tinderbox waiting to explode. The atmosphere was fraught with tension and uneasiness as the people of France boiled with anger and exasperation at the despotic reign of the monarchy.

The teeming crowds of people gathered in the streets and stayed there as the evening turned into night. One could see their faces lit up by the flames of the flickering torches they carried. The clamor of their angry voices echoed off the walls of the city as they shouted vociferous slogans and called for change. It was as if they could sense change was on the horizon.

Amidst the pandemonium, there were groups of people at peace, but their hearts were filled with a profound sense of fear and uncertainty. Mothers clutched their offspring, their eyes scanning the mob for any sign of danger. Elderly men watched with a mix of acceptance and despair, while young men and women were filled with a ferocious determination to fight for their rights.

The tension was tangible, and the crowd surged forward, the people's fists raised in defiance. One could hear the explosive sounds of shattering glass and the stench of burning wood. Shuttered windows were broken open, and doors were smashed in. The smell of burning flesh and smoke filled the air as small fires turned into large bonfires in the street as the crowd moved toward the Bastille to gain weapons and gunpowder that were stored there.

As the night progressed, the chaos only increased. The shouts of scared men and women mingled with the sounds of gunshots piercing through the darkness. The forces of the monarchy clashed with the revolutionary mobs, and the streets flowed with blood.

It was a scene of absolute chaos and devastation. The people of France had suddenly woken from their cozy slumber and seemed determined to fight for their rights.

The French Revolution had begun. And the world would never be the same again.

King Louis and Marie Antoinette

King Louis XVI was the king of France when the French Revolution took place in 1789. He married Marie Antoinette of Austria for political reasons when he was only fifteen. He became king in 1774 at the tender age of nineteen. Louis was an intellectually capable person, but he lacked decisiveness and authority. However, he was still an absolute monarch, and his rule has often been regarded as corrupt and extravagant.

Still, he made sweeping reforms in all areas of the government, including religion, foreign policy, and financial matters. He signed the 1787 Edict of Versailles, which gave non-Catholics civil and legal status in France and the opportunity to practice their faith. He likely could have been considered an enlightened ruler if it were not for the crippling debt France had incurred. His financial reforms to get France out of debt were blocked by the nobles and *parlements*. Few understood the state's dire financial situation, and matters got worse by the day.

King Louis XVI and Queen Marie Antoinette lived in the luxurious Palace of Versailles, away from the problems of the masses. As discontent grew, King Louis did little to understand the economic and financial troubles of his people.

Marie Antoinette's wasteful lifestyle particularly irked the people. In 1789, after being told that the French population was facing a shortage of bread and was starving because of the poor crop harvest, Marie

Antoinette famously exclaimed, "Let them eat cake!" It is widely believed that she never uttered these words; the idea that she said them appeared decades after her death. However, the people knew she spent enormous sums on dresses and games when they could barely afford to buy bread.

The Palace of Versailles was stormed by an angry mob on October 5th, 1789. The royal family was captured and taken to Paris, where they were forced to accept their new roles as constitutional monarchs. After nearly two years of negotiations, Louis and his family attempted to flee Paris for Varennes, but their plan failed, and they were recaptured. Louis was put on trial for high treason. He was executed by guillotine on January 21st, 1793.

His wife, Marie Antoinette, was executed nearly ten months later, on October 16th, 1793. Louis's death marked the end of over one thousand years of a continuous monarchy. Many have argued it was a key moment in the radicalization of revolutionary violence.

The French Revolution

You might be wondering why we are talking about the French Revolution in a book on the Enlightenment. Well, the French Revolution might have never occurred if it were not for the Enlightenment. And it was essentially Enlightenment thoughts put into action. The cries for equality, freedom, and brotherhood reverberated through the streets of Paris and beyond as the insurgents battled to form a new society based on those principles.

At the center of the French Revolution was a profound sense of injustice and subjugation felt by the masses. The catalyst was the famine and shortage of grain due to poor crops and pests. The insurgents faced formidable adversaries, including the aristocracy, the church, and foreign powers, all of whom were resolute in maintaining the status quo. But despite the odds, the insurgents, driven by a deep sense of resolve and a conviction in their cause, persevered.

The French Revolution started on May 5th, 1789, with the summoning of the Estates General. Representatives from the three estates of French society—the clergy, the nobility, and the common people—gathered together upon orders of the king, Louis XVI, to address the growing financial crisis in the country. The Estates General had not assembled since 1614.

Although the Third Estate had been promised more representation, they soon found out the promised representation would not be enough to outweigh the votes of the First Estate, whose members held contrasting views on what would be best for France. So, instead of debating with the other two estates, the Third Estate met on its own, eventually declaring itself to be the National Assembly.

The National Assembly invited the other estates to join but also warned them that they would continue with their goals, with or without them. King Louis XVI unsurprisingly did not like this turn of events, as he could see that power was slipping out of his fingers. Although he tried to shut the National Assembly down, he could not. And as time passed, members from the other estates (mainly the Second Estate) joined the National Assembly, calling for a constitution.

The king sent out the military, hoping to rein in the people's passion. However, this move only served to upset them more. They demanded the king remove the military, but the king refused, instead offering to move the National Assembly to a safer place, one where they would be cut off from the people of Paris.

Things escalated until the storming of the Bastille occurred on July 14th, 1789. As mentioned above, the Bastille was a fortress and prison in Paris that had come to signify the tyranny of the monarchy. At the time, the prison only had seven inmates, but the people weren't there to free political prisoners. Instead, the event was supposed to be a symbolic attack on the monarchy. The Bastille also gave the mob armor, weaponry, and ammunition.

The storming of the Bastille is seen as the starting point of the French Revolution. The people wanted to reform the government, create a constitution, and provide the people with basic liberties. The idea should sound familiar, as this was something Enlightenment thinkers often wrote about. The Americans' victory over the British was also one of the catalysts for the French Revolution. The French people saw that a revolt could be successful, even against a major military power. Although the American government was new at that time, the French saw the potential for a reformed government and the promises that it could bring.

The Declaration of the Rights of Man and of the Citizen was ratified on October 5th, 1789, by Louis XVI under pressure from the riots that had broken out. This document served as the preamble to the first constitution in 1791.

The Declaration of the Rights of Man and of the Citizen was inspired by the writings of Enlightenment philosophers, such as Jean-Jacques Rousseau, Montesquieu, and Voltaire. Other influences included the 1776 Virginia Declaration of Rights and the manifesto of the Dutch Patriot movement of the 1780s. The creators of the Declaration went beyond its sources, as they intended the principles to be universally applicable.

The Declaration has a preamble and seventeen brief articles. The first article contains the document's central statement: "Men are born and remain free and equal in rights." It states that the purpose of "political association" should be the preservation of these rights, with those rights being "liberty, property, security, and resistance to oppression." The document protects the freedom of speech and religion and also provides equal treatment of people before the law. It also asserts that taxes should be paid by all citizens in accordance with their means.

Things were fairly peaceful until Louis XVI and his family tried to escape. People were worried that spies and traitors were among them, causing distrust. Faction groups rose up, threatening the unity of the revolution. Other monarchs, fearing that the revolution would spread, declared their support for Louis. Some even hinted at invading France to help stop the revolt.

Progress needed to be made, and the French formed the Legislative Assembly in October 1791. However, this assembly was not very strong. For the most part, it ignored the people the French Revolution was fighting for: the working class, those who were the most affected by the bread shortages. There were also those who felt the French Revolution had gone too far; these people were likely shocked at how much further it would go.

The French Revolutionary Wars began in April 1792, with French forces fighting Austrians and Prussians who were situated along the border. The French were not very successful at first, but the Brunswick Manifesto, whose details were revealed in early August, angered the French. The manifesto stated that if the royal family were harmed, then civilians would be harmed. Obviously, the manifesto was supposed to intimidate the people into submission. But it had the opposite effect. Later that month, Louis was removed from the throne. About a month later, the French First Republic replaced the monarchy.

Things quickly escalated after this. For instance, in September, over one thousand prisoners in jails were executed, as they were thought to be potentially conspiring with Prussia. In January 1793, Louis XVI was condemned to death, a move that horrified the European monarchs.

It was clear by this point that the French Revolution had morphed into something that went against the "ideal" Enlightenment thoughts. It is very likely that Enlightenment thinkers would have been shocked at the brutality that occurred. But reality is often different than lofty thoughts dreamed up in some salon. The dates for the Reign of Terror differ, with some pointing to the September Massacre as the beginning or to 1793 when the Revolutionary Tribunal was formed. Regardless of when it started, it was a period of intense violence, turmoil, and political oppression. Around seventeen thousand perceived adversaries of the French Revolution were killed, while another ten thousand died in prison.

The Reign of Terror was led by Jacobin leader Maximilien Robespierre. He pointed to the ideas brought up during the Enlightenment to encourage the people, saying that a government should act for the good of the people instead of certain groups. However, Robespierre believed that the only way that could happen was by expelling those who fought against such an idea. In his opinion, terror was the only way to create the kind of France he envisioned.

Robespierre had many goals he wanted to accomplish, such as the right for people of color and Jews to vote. He wanted to end the slave trade in France and give men the right to bear arms for self-defense. During the Reign of Terror, Maximilien Robespierre gained immense power. He was brutal and caused fear, but in his mind, he was doing it for the good of his country. However, personal rivalries and clashes with other revolutionaries contributed to his downfall, resulting in his arrest and execution in July 1794.

In 1795, the Directory was established, along with a new constitution. The Directory was a five-man executive committee that brought about a period of relative political stability. However, the Directory was unable to tackle the ongoing political and economic problems of France. Some saw the group as a betrayal of what they had been fighting for. It was dissolved by a coup by Napoleon Bonaparte in 1799.

Napoleon created the Consulate, which was composed of three assemblies. Even so, Napoleon held a lot of power. In 1802, he declared himself First Consul for Life, a role that is akin to a dictator. Although the French Revolution succeeded in establishing a republic in 1792, that republic was torn down when Napoleon Bonaparte was crowned the emperor of France in 1804.

Napoleon Bonaparte

Napoleon Bonaparte is an interesting figure in history, and he is considered an enlightened autocrat, so his background is worth exploring. He was born on the island of Corsica in 1769, the same year Corsica became a French territory. Napoleon was picked on in school because of his accent and birthplace. He became very introverted, devoting himself to his studies.

And his hard work paid off. He started his career as a second lieutenant in the French Army in 1785. Because of his expertise in military matters, he rose through the ranks, and by 1793, he had become a general.

During the French Revolution, Napoleon played a pivotal role in several campaigns, and he swiftly gained notoriety as an ingenious martial strategist. In 1796, he led the French Army to triumph in Italy, and he followed this up with a sequence of campaigns in Egypt and Syria, which were not as successful.

Napoleon made sure to keep on what was happening in France while he was on campaign in Egypt. Worried that France would be lost after hearing about its defeats in the French Revolutionary Wars, he sailed back to France, even though he did not receive orders to do so. By the time he had arrived, the situation had stabilized, but it was clear to Napoleon that the Directory was not fit to lead; it couldn't even properly punish him for deserting his men.

Perhaps that is when the wheels started turning in Napoleon's mind. He met with other influential figures to discuss a coup, which happened in November 1799. He became the First Consul for ten years, but he later decided to extend that term for life. And then he went one step further and declared himself emperor.

As emperor, Napoleon enforced a sequence of far-reaching reforms that transformed France into a contemporary, centralized state. He created a new judicial system called the Napoleonic Code, which created equality before the law and secured the people's rights to property. He also changed the educational infrastructure, instituted a system of civic projects, and propagated economic expansion and growth. He created the first central bank and sought to ease tensions with the Catholic Church, whose clergymen had been targeted during the French Revolution. Of course, like any enlightened despot, Napoleon had his downfalls. One of the most notable tyrannical things he did was reinstate slavery in the Caribbean. It ultimately did not matter for the people in Haiti, who were able to rise up and create their own government without slavery in 1804. Although Napoleon later abolished the slave trade during the Hundred Days, his legacy regarding slavery is not seen in a favorable light.

Napoleon's military conquests expanded the limits of France, but in doing so, he made a lot of enemies, primarily Britain. Today, Napoleon is seen as a military genius, with his battles and tactics studied by military scholars and buffs. He did suffer defeats, but with a military career of over eighty battles and only losing eleven of those battles is pretty good. Nevertheless, he was eventually defeated in 1814 and forced to relinquish his throne. He was exiled to the island of Elba.

However, Napoleon was not content to sit still. He returned to France in 1815, where he briefly regained authority in a phase recognized as the Hundred Days. He was famously defeated in the Battle of Waterloo in June 1815, and he was exiled again, this time to the island of Saint Helena in the South Atlantic. There, he died as a prisoner in 1821 at the relatively young age of fifty-one. The end of the Napoleonic Wars is typically used as a convenient end date for the Enlightenment, although some argue that it ended earlier.

Conclusion

The Age of Enlightenment was a period of transformation, a time when rationality and personal autonomy were embraced. Enlightenment philosophers believed in the right to life, freedom, and ownership of property. They championed the concept of democracy and the rule of law. They also believed that government should be based on the consent of the governed and that laws should be created through a logical and democratic process.

The Enlightenment gave birth to a world that was completely different from anything that existed before. Inventions and discoveries were made that changed how people saw the world. Ideas about new forms of governance challenged the status quo and forced the people to think more critically. Women made a push to be seen and heard in different ways than before, laying the groundwork for future suffragist movements. The Enlightenment changed many things, but it mainly provided the foundation for a new world, a world that was secular, experimental, individualistic, and, above all, progressive.

It is rather difficult to imagine how the world would have turned out without the Enlightenment since it was a complex movement that had a far-reaching impact in many different fields. However, we can make some educated guesses.

Without the Enlightenment, the values of liberty, separate branches of government, and religious tolerance would not have been as deeply ingrained in Western culture as they are today. Religious and superstitious beliefs might have had a much greater impact on people's thinking today. Scientific progress and technological innovations might not have advanced as astonishingly as they did.

Without an emphasis on empirical reasoning and experimentation, our comprehension of the natural world might be much more limited today. For instance, we might have never discovered insulin or learned about the structure of the atom.

Without the influence of Enlightenment thinkers like John Locke and Montesquieu, many countries would likely still be ruled by dictators or monarchs, and the concept of human rights would not have gained the widespread acceptance it has today.

And the absence of fundamental rights would have meant a legal system that didn't benefit the people. This hypothetical legal system likely would not have placed importance on the protection of the accused, making it difficult for individuals to prove their innocence. Laws in many countries might have heavily tilted in favor of the state, making it easier for authorities to imprison or torture citizens and even entire families. Punishments would likely have been more severe, with people being sentenced to long, inhumane prison sentences and barbaric forms of execution.

The impact of the Enlightenment on the modern world cannot be overstated. It was a period of great excitement, where thinkers of all kinds gathered to question the old ways of thinking and created new pathways to a more reasonable, humane society.

These concepts greatly influenced the revolutions in France and the United States. After all, the Declaration of Independence was based heavily on Enlightenment philosophy, particularly the philosophy of John Locke, who believed that every individual had a right to life, freedom, and ownership of property. The French Revolution sought liberty, equality, and brotherhood. These concepts and values were directly inspired by Enlightenment thinkers like Rousseau and Voltaire.

Without the Enlightenment, these revolutions might not have occurred or might have created something entirely different. Would Thomas Jefferson have been inspired to write the Declaration of Independence without John Locke's thoughts to guide him? Would the French have rebelled just to replace their ruler with another king? These are, of course, hypotheticals, but they are interesting to think about.

While it is difficult to argue for certain what would have occurred without the Enlightenment, it is clear that the ideas and values of the Enlightenment had a profound impact on history.

Here's another book by Enthralling History that you might like

Free limited time bonus

Stop for a moment. We have a free bonus set up for you. The problem is this: we forget 90% of everything that we read after 7 days. Crazy fact, right? Here's the solution: we've created a printable, 1-page pdf summary for this book that you're reading now. All you have to do to get your free pdf summary is to go to the following website:

https://livetolearn.lpages.co/enthrallinghistory/

Once you do, it will be intuitive. Enjoy, and thank you!

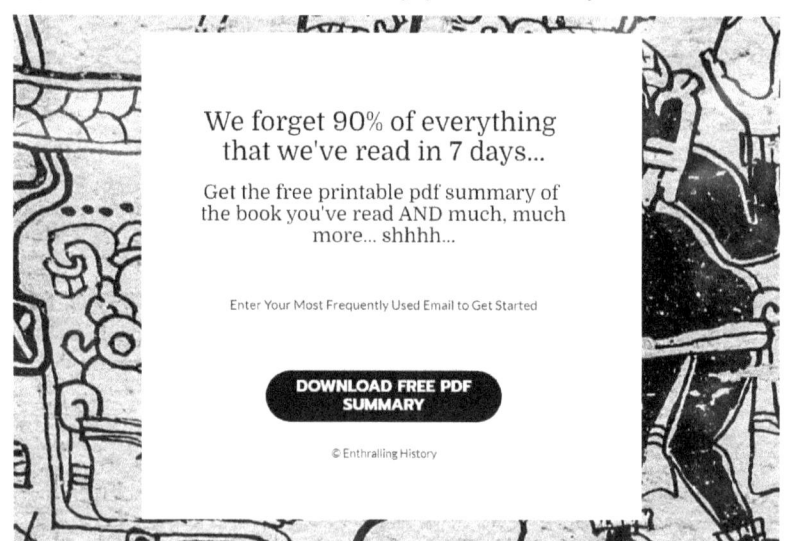

Bibliography

The Internet Encyclopedia of Philosophy
https://iep.utm.edu/
Britannica
https://www.britannica.com/
Stanford Encyclopedia of Philosophy
https://plato.stanford.edu/
Reill, Peter Hanns (2004), Encyclopedia of the Enlightenment, New York, Facts On File, Inc.
S. Pinker (2018) Enlightenment Now, New York, Penguin Random House.
A, Gottlieb, (2016) The Dream Of Enlightenment. New York, W. W. Norton & Co.
A, Gottlieb, (2016) The Dream Of Reason, New York, W. W. Norton & Co.
V. Ferrone, (2015) The Enlightenment, New Jersey, Princeton University Press
S. Fleischacker, (2013) What is Enlightenment?, New York, Routledge
R. Wokler (2001) Rousseau, A Very Short Introduction, New York, Oxford University Press
A.J. Ayer (2000) Hume, A Very Short Introduction, New York, Oxford University Press
John Dunn (1984) Locke, A Very Short Introduction, New York, Oxford University Press
Roger Scruton (1986) Spinoza, A Short Introduction, New York, Oxford University Press

www.ingramcontent.com/pod-product-compliance
Lightning Source LLC
Chambersburg PA
CBHW070340010526
44107CB00004B/574